Earl Marshal School, Sheffield, February 1993: students demonstrate in support of miners, with National Union of Mineworkers official. Photograph by courtesy of Sheffield Newspapers Ltd

NONE BUT OUR WORDS

Critical literacy in classroom and community

CHRIS SEARLE

'None but ourselves can free our minds:'
[Bob Marley]

Open University Press
Buckingham • Philadelphia

Open University Press
Celtic Court
22 Ballmoor
Buckingham
MK18 1XW

email: enquiries@openup.co.uk
world wide web: http://www.openup.co.uk

and
325 Chestnut Street
Philadelphia, PA 19106, USA

First Published 1998

A catalogue record of this book is available from the British Library

ISBN 0 335 20127 X (pb)   0 335 20128 8 (hb)

Library of Congress Cataloging-in-Publication Data

Searle, Chris.
    None but our words : critical literacy in classroom and community
/ Chris Searle.
       p. cm.
    Includes bibliographical references and index.
    ISBN 0-335-20128-8 (hardcover). — ISBN 0-335-20127-X (pbk.)
    1. Language arts—Social aspects—Great Britain.   2. Literacy—
Social aspects—Great Britain.   3. Critical pedagogy—Great
Britain.   I. Title.
LB1631.S454   1998
428'.0071'2—dc21   97–46655
                                                                  CIP

Typeset by Graphicraft Typesetters Ltd, Hong Kong
Printed in Great Britain by Biddles Ltd, Guildford and Kings Lynn

CONTENTS

FOREWORD: THE CULTURAL POLITICS OF CLASSROOM LIFE

COLIN LANKSHEAR

I

None But Our Words is a classic text in the radical educational tradition. It is in fact a wonderfully coherent marshalling of myriad texts produced by many different people which, as the word radical implies, takes us to the very roots of education as social practice. Chris Searle does not write as an individual but rather as a representative of his social class and its educational tradition. Moreover, and in accordance with that position, he writes in the company of others. His texts typically mobilize many voices – past and present, from near and afar – many representatives of the working-class tradition, which is in the final analysis and necessarily, a tradition of solidarity, of people addressing the world together. This latest book portrays working-class education through prose, letters, poems and passages of reported speech. The pages are alive with vibrant words, evocative and colourful thoughts, expressions of aspiring and indomitable spirits, and of the will to dignity, respect, and mutual good will. It is an inspiring read.

Of course, the tradition of working-class education, like working-class politics more generally, is a tradition of struggle from a position of inferior power. From the earliest times of mass schooling, working-class education has been the site of contest between competing forces. On one side are those who champion working-class education in terms of the right to a just share of the social wage, in order that working people might become – as Paulo Freire[1] puts it – all that their humanity permits and demands, and to do so on equal terms with all others. On the opposite side are those for whom working-class education is necessary in order to maintain states of affairs which best serve

the interests of social elites. This is an educational tradition based on social-
izing subordinate social groups to become 'beings for others': fitted to occupy
subordinate places in established social, cultural, and political hierarchies.
Often the contest looks like no contest at all, the working-class side confined
to student expressions of boredom, disaffection and alienation, with occasional protests from working communities about the physical condition of
local schools, low morale and poor results. At such times it takes genuinely
effective counter-cultural educational practice on behalf of the educational
interests of subordinate social groups to bring the reality of working-class
education as contested terrain out into the open. *None But Our Words* documents telling moments of such counter-cultural practice. The period of almost
30 years spanned by the various texts assembled between the covers of this
book is recounted in terms of critical pedagogical activity within classrooms
of working-class and minority linguistic and ethnic-cultural groups, meeting
with polarized responses as it reached levels of visibility and effectiveness in
the public sphere.

As a whole, *None But Our Words* represents a vibrant case study of the
cultural politics of education. It describes 'pedagogy against the grain' occur-
ring within classrooms, and the kind of learning that can go on under such
conditions. At the same time, it describes what can happen to people, to
learning, to schools and to entire communities, when those whose interests
lie 'with the grain' have their comfort unsettled, disrupted. This is an unsettling book. It challenges us at every point to own up to where we stand, to
decide what we believe about and want for education, and how far we are
prepared to struggle for our ideals. How much of the world are we prepared
to admit into our classrooms? How far are we prepared to extend our classroom learning out into the world beyond, and to allow the learners in our
charge to locate and name the issues that properly concern active citizens in
search of a just and peaceful world, citizens who understand that the one is
a precondition of the other?

II

None But Our Words is a vital book right now. It
should be widely read by tomorrow's teachers who are currently receiving
their pre-service teacher education. Likewise, teachers who are already in
service can learn much from this book, and take heart from the courage and
integrity it exemplifies. Nobody who reads this book could possibly leave its
pages without having grasped, in highly graphic ways, the extent to which
genuine alternatives *do* exist in education generally, and literacy education
specifically; that the interests of different groups are served differently by the
alternatives that win out in education; that, for precisely this reason, education is political; and that building and bringing alternative educational visions to fruition requires struggling for them – and sometimes, in the short
run, we do not win. How long that short run is depends on how many
others share our vision and are prepared to struggle with us. If there was ever
a time for teachers and other educators to struggle over and for education,
that time is surely now.

Activities which probe and discuss the inescapably *political* nature and context of schooling have become highly marginalized within teacher education and professional development programmes. This is by no means simply a result of decisions by teacher educators as to what is important and not important. Teacher education students and teachers in service are often quick to challenge the relevance of courses and professional development components that do not seem to have immediately apparent 'face validity': that do not provide 'tricks' for teaching reading and writing, templates for lesson planning and programming, formulae for scope and sequence and devices for managing behaviour in class. Understandably, they want control of *technique* first and foremost.

While regrettable, this is hardly surprising within societies dominated by 'technological rationality' – the belief that technique provides the answer to practically every significant question. In addition of course, faith in techniques and insistence on programmes which purvey them are bolstered by the demanding conditions under which many teachers work. These include burgeoning class sizes, diverse and complex student populations, unfriendly public perceptions of teachers and teaching, a 'hungry' and often hostile media, intensified teacher work (which now includes seemingly endless administrivia which, for many teachers, is quite alienating), and highly visible and regulated reporting and accountability regimes which double as sophisticated surveillance and regulatory mechanisms for the state. Given such conditions it is hardly surprising that teacher educators and 'teachers in training' assign the status and urgency they do to matters of technique and content.

Yet, sometimes the fastest way to a destination involves taking the longer road. Learning techniques and proliferating content 'knowledge' run a poor second to mastering principles and acquiring capacities for understanding, inferring, interpreting and researching, that enable us to create, modify, refine and generate specific techniques and content as *culturally and critically informed* responses to pedagogical and administrative situations *as they arise*. These latter capacities, after all, are the sorts of things supposed to mark the distinction between teacher *training* and teacher *education*. It is ironic that our rhetoric of the present – it's a 'meta age'; we need 'knowledge workers'; 'higher order skills' are the clue to success and survival in the information age – is largely belied by everyday practice in contexts where mechanistic conceptions of skill and measurable competence grab the headlines and dominate so much educational policy.

In *Lives on the Boundary*, Mike Rose names the politics of preference currently playing out at the pressure points of policy and practice within language and literacy education in stark and compelling terms. He refers back to a 'model' of pedagogical effectiveness developed earlier this century under the dual tutelage of positivist approaches to educational research and the desire to apply principles of industrial scientific management to education in the name of efficiency. Rose looks at how this 'model' was taken up within language and literacy education. He describes the approach of educational researchers to language as 'a mechanistic orientation that studied language by reducing it to discrete behaviors and that defined growth as the accretion of particulars'.[2] This meshed well with the ethos of scientific management, in terms of which 'educational gains were defined as products, and the output of products could be measured'.[3] The upshot of this was a conception of pedagogical effectiveness equating with cost-effectiveness, and which could be determined with 'scientific accuracy'. What finally emerged, says Rose, was 'a conception of positivism, efficiency, and a focus on grammar that would have a profound influence on [language and literacy] pedagogy'.[4]

The dominance of this broad model lives on, in the guise of school effectiveness and improvement, and in fact is in rampant ascendance at present. While US education may have received a more concentrated dose of it than emerged in Britain and such colonial outposts as Australasia and Canada, its influence was none the less considerable in those systems, and has surfaced with a vengeance in full-blown form during the past decade. Yet the model has been subjected to serious challenges throughout most of its 'career': challenges from language and literacy teachers as well as from theory and theory-driven research. There exists a large body of thought and literature arguing the poverty of mechanistic and narrowly quantitative approaches to language and literacy, replete with powerful refutations of abstracted, a-cultural, one-dimensional mechanistic conceptions of language. Even so, the largely discredited 'model' lives on, *officially*, and at no time more visibly, explicitly and powerfully than right now. Why?

Here again Rose explains the situation as clearly and accurately as can be. He says:

> This trend has the staying power it does for a number of reasons. It gives a method – a putatively objective one – to the strong desire . . . to maintain correct language use . . . And it offers a simple, understandable view of complex linguistic problems. The trend reemerges most forcefully in times of crisis: when budgets crunch and accountability looms or, particularly, when 'non traditional' students flood our institutions. A reduction of complexity has great appeal in institutional decision making, especially in difficult times: a scientific-atomistic approach to language, with its attendant tallies and charts, nicely fits an economic decision-making model. When in doubt or when scared or when pressed, count.[5]

And when the figures don't 'compute', count some more – *diagnose and 'remediate'*. And count the results here as well.

At a time when opponents of sociocultural and critical approaches to education line up to announce rampant illiteracy as the number one growth industry of our schools, technicist 'quick fixes', admixed with good square doses of 'skills' bolstered by mandatory tests at regular age intervals, become the order of the day for all – including especially, for students who encounter standard English as a second, third, or more distantly ordered language. *None But Our Words* establishes the case, beyond reasonable doubt, that far richer and more effective approaches to language and literacy learning than the official variant are available for challenging widely-perceived and publicized patterns of 'educational disadvantage' and 'endemic underachievement' among working-class/ESL-migrant students.

One crucial feature of *None But Our Words* is that it is not soft on rigorously pursuing mastery of literacy skills and techniques *per se*. Searle advocates the utmost importance of controlling skills, techniques and accuracy and advocates it directly and explicitly. What marks Searle off from their narrow technicist advocates is that he simply *refuses* to abstract these dimensions from the larger and richer character of language and literacy. Searle insists on addressing skills, techniques and accuracy in terms of their embeddedness within larger social and cultural practices, and in terms of the relationship between the myriad literacies embedded in social-cultural practices and access to life chances. From the very outset of his career as a teacher, Chris Searle has maintained consistently that working-class children should learn to read and write, spell and punctuate, and develop the word as a tool. His point, however, is that learners should develop the word as a tool within a larger social, cultural and political context.

This is a context of struggle on the part of subordinated and marginalized groups for improvement and liberation: their own as well as that of people like them, wherever they may live. In the final analysis, developing the word as a tool for improvement and liberation is embedded in a politics of solidarity. Local efforts to master literacy are pursued in the context of social practices which have international as well as more localized referents – precisely because improvement and liberation are universal ideals, not the property of particular groups only. For this reason the World must come into the literacy classroom. Not the World in a sanitized form, however, but the World as *ideological*: the World as the expression and creation of social and cultural practices which bestow 'social goods' (status, comfort, dignity, money, opportunities, power) *differentially* – more to some and less to others.[6] Just as language and literacy are integral to the social practices which create the World as it is, so they are integral to social practices that can transform that World in the direction of a more just and equal distribution of 'goods'. Foremost among these 'goods' is the right – the opportunity and power – to have an equal say with all other human beings as to what the World should *be*: that is, an equal right to 'name the World'.[7]

III

None But Our Words has much to contribute to the education of language and literacy teachers who are already in classrooms as well as those in the making. It goes far beyond providing a checklist of techniques and formulae for teaching the Word. By the same token, discerning readers will discover a rich store of practical procedures, techniques and wisdom along the way.

The book is an inspiring multi-voiced narrative of vital everyday struggles within the cultural politics of school education. It draws on the words and work of diverse people who between them, represent key players in the education arena. This is an arena where contests are waged daily around what will be learned, how it will be learned, what learning is for, who will get to learn what, who will teach it, under what conditions, and who gets to decide all these things.

In the following pages we encounter the words of *students*, mainly conveyed as poems and stretches of prose produced as classroom literacy work, but also, occasionally, as reported in media accounts of episodes in the 'curriculum and pedagogy struggles' which comprise the thematic heart of *None But Our Words*. We encounter the words of *politicians* and *administrators* who sense what is at stake in education. *Parents* and *citizens*, particularly from urban working-class and migrant communities, also speak to us here – in private and public capacities – about their educational values and hopes. *Media commentators* on education, *journalists*, and various *public intellectuals* (including the occasional poet and exponents of other literary genres) also enter the fray and declare their positions on the proper business of schooling. *Teachers* and *principals*, of course, are here as well, and very much in the foreground. For this book is an account of educational politics focused on events and episodes originating in classroom and school communities inhabited by the author – and other like-minded teachers – but which burst dynamically, graphically, and profoundly into public spaces where educational work in schools ultimately bears its fruits.

As Paulo Freire, quintessential educator of the people worldwide, often reminded us, 'Word' is simultaneously 'Work'. Words do not live and die unto themselves but, rather, enact effects in the 'World'. As Chris Searle observes in the opening lines of his Introduction, 'words are the forerunners and prompters of action, [hence] the teaching of words cannot be separated from encouragement to action'. The words narrated in this text from the different perspectives of their speakers chronicle work done in the world: work which makes education and learning what they are, and what they are not, in specific sites. *None But Our Words* portrays the work of people in different capacities playing roles which influence the shape of education within the society. It leaves us in no doubt that education is not and cannot be *neutral*.

Schooling is inevitably among the most powerful forces shaping what people can become. It is not, however, an autonomous force acting independently. Rather it is inescapably linked to work done within other sites of human practice. To this extent it is also linked to the interests, aspirations, values, actions, beliefs, purposes, ideals, visions, goals, commitments, and wills of those human beings involved in the myriad social practices engaged within those sites. These are the very social practices which, collectively constitute 'the World'. What goes on in classrooms is inevitably imprinted by what goes on elsewhere, just as what goes on elsewhere is inevitably imprinted by the work done in classrooms. *None But Our Words* shows through the life work and words of everyday players on the educational stage how schooling is inescapably involved in contributing to the creation and maintenance of one kind of World or another.

It is not as if there is some kind of pre-given world which education somehow operates within as a neutral tool, technology, or instrument. The impossibility of schooling having a neutral role here applies at two levels.

The first is that schooling itself is part of the very process of making and remaking the world. It simply cannot 'get' outside of that process. Rather, its 'choice' is about what kind of world it will be conducive to making – and, correspondingly, what kinds of worlds it will be conducive to 'thwarting'. The second level at which schooling cannot be neutral has to do with its role in helping to uphold or transform those effects upon human possibilities that are contingent upon the world being the way it is (or isn't). The world that schooling contributes to building under current economic and social conditions is *the same world* that allocates and withholds social goods to individuals and groups differentially. Hence, what goes on in classrooms is not neutral, *and cannot be neutral*, with respect to those differential allocations and withholdings of goods. It either takes a stand *against* larger practices of hierarchy and differential allocation of goods, or it goes along with them. To be 'not against' is, at the very least, to be 'complicit with'. Chris Searle's approach as a teacher has always been to encourage students to recognize unjust allocations of social goods, and to explore approaches to social practice which reject and transcend injustices, inequities, and indifference to them.

What unfolds on the pages of *None But Our Words* is a fascinating account of how Searle's attempts to make education into such a social practice of words and deeds have consistently been attacked by various forces over almost thirty years, on the grounds that they are not neutral; on the grounds that they are ideological and, even, *indoctrinatory*. Those who advance these judgments do so from the assumption that what *they* propose, practise, and uphold *is* neutral, and is *not* ideological or indoctrinatory. This is a powerful political manoeuvre. Its logic is quite simple, yet it seems to fool many of us much of the time. Those who assume the right and the capacity to speak on behalf of 'educational truth' assert their own position as being proper and, to that extent, 'given'. They assert it, in other words, as being some kind of pre-given 'baseline' comprising a normal or proper state of affairs. From this it seems to follow that anyone who gets out of line is, by definition – and granted the premise – behaving non-neutrally. They are said to be taking up a stance, and the moment they adopt and act on this stance in a classroom they are said to be engaging in manipulation, indoctrination, and even subversion. At the very least, they are being 'ideological', and behaving 'ideologically'. On the other hand, those who (claim to) represent the 'natural' or 'proper' state of affairs proclaim themselves *not* to be taking up a stance, and are widely *seen* not to be taking up a stance – and hence, *not* to be engaging in, or otherwise supporting, forms of manipulation, indoctrination, or ideology.

The facts of the matter are, of course, that these critics *are* taking up a stance. In particular, they are taking up a stance against ideas and practices being engaged in classrooms that question the ways power, wealth, status, opportunities and life chances, adequate housing, dignity, academic achievement, and many other social goods are currently allocated – and that question the bases on which these allocations are made. Yet, surely to remain stuck unquestioningly inside everyday assumptions about such things as the inevitability of some people having more than others, or the 'fact' that certain languages/dialects (standard English and English standards) are superior to others and certain domains of knowledge more 'educational' than others, or that to be part of a nation means subordinating cultural and ethnic diversity to principles of 'One Nationhood', is precisely what it means to be 'indoctrinated' or, at least, ideologically hoodwinked.

As Jim Gee observes, learning works 'best', in the sense of being 'most enculturating', when it is done *inside* the social practices of Discourses. But, when learning works 'best' in this sense it is also at its 'most indoctrinating'.[8] Unfortunately, that is precisely what many of Searle's critics are advocating. They are content for classroom learning to go on *inside* the social practices of particular Discourses. Indeed, they *insist* on learning going on inside the social practices of particular Discourses. These include established Discourses of curriculum – which, we must remember, involve selections from a culture, but whose selections and whose/which culture, and on what basis, and to whose greater benefit? – meritocracy, nationhood/allegiance, citizenship and so on. Where the work of teachers like Searle rankles with his opponents is where it creates opportunities for students to question some of the very assumptions of these established Discourses; to be encouraged to look at everyday events and phenomena from different perspectives; to test conventional assumptions against empirical experience; to explore different cultural values and to imagine different realities; to put themselves in the positions of other people and to imagine what the world looks like from their positions; to explore whether or not our dominant sources of knowledge and wisdom, such as the mass media, politicians, clergy, and other 'officials', are delivering us 'the truth'. Ironically, in encouraging students to try on different perspectives, Searle and others like him are actually striking a blow *against* everyday forms and practices of indoctrination; and in discouraging teachers like Searle from doing this, his detractors are striking a blow *for* everyday forms and practices of indoctrination.

IV

Chris Searle describes *None But Our Words* as looking back at 'the various classroom initiatives of critical literacy with which I have been involved', and the responses to these initiatives (p. 3). He adds:

> I have always taught working-class and black students, either in the British inner city, the Caribbean or Africa. My perspectives have been formed through that experience and a working commitment towards those communities, and a wish, with them, to see their children prosper and take power in the world which is theirs.

This link between critical literacy and taking power is absolutely central to Searle's identity and work as an educator. We can clarify the issues raised in the previous section and situate them in a larger frame by asking what the practice of a critical, *powerful* literacy involves. In my view, critical literacy involves literacy practices which engage us in a critique of Discourses that regulate who and what we become individually and collectively. The agenda underlying this view assumes that discursive constructions of the good life are provisional, that to be educated is to be capable of critiquing dominant Discourses, and that it is the right of every person to be educated in this sense.

In the pages that follow, Chris Searle takes us on a narrative journey of how he essays the tasks inherent in such an ideal of critical literacy and powerful learning. As we read the words of the many participants in this narrative, and the counternarratives raised against it, we will be able to explore in new ways what is at issue in being an educator, and what rides on the decisions we make, the options we choose, and those we do not make or choose. Engaging actively and critically with the ideas and challenges presented in *None But Our Words* will contribute much to our continuing education and growth as educators. The invitation and opportunity to do this is Chris Searle's gift to us, his colleagues and peers. He does not ask us to agree with him, let alone to agree with him unquestioningly. He does, however, quietly hope that we will open ourselves to feeling, understanding and grappling with the tensions and struggles that inevitably accompany the vocation of being an educator in a world where allocations and distributions of social goods are becoming less equitable by the day, and, in *feeling* those tensions, to resolve to face and address them square on and from an ethical point of view.

After all, if we are not prepared to do that, we should not be in education.

Colin Lankshear
Brisbane

Notes

1 Paulo Freire, *Pedagogy of the Oppressed*, Penguin, 1972.
2 Michael Rose, *Lives on the Boundary: The Struggles and Achievements of America's Underprepared*, The Free Press, 1989.
3 *Lives on the Boundary*, p. 208, ibid.
4 *Lives on the Boundary*, p. 208, ibid.
5 *Lives on the Boundary*, pp. 208–9, ibid.
6 J.P. Gee, *Social Linguistics and Literacies: Ideology in Discourses*, Chapter 1, 2nd edition, Taylor & Francis, 1996.
7 Paulo Freire, *Pedagogy of the Oppressed*, Penguin, 1972.
8 J.P. Gee, G. Hull and C. Lankshear, *The New Work Order: Behind the Language of the New Capitalism*, p. 15, Allen & Unwin and Westview Press, 1996.

ACKNOWLEDGEMENTS

None But Our Words contains the work of many people with whom I have worked through three decades of teaching. I thank them, and hope that at some point they will encounter their words again within these pages.

I would like to thank Pearl, and our sons Victor, Kevin, Daniel and Russell for their help and support, and the latter three for their computer skills (though not always for their spelling!). Thanks too, to my two dear colleagues Colin Lankshear and Mike Apple for their fine contributions and to Shona Mullen and her colleagues at Open University Press for their hard work.

None But Our Words was completed in the year of the death of the great Brazilian literacy educator and human of the world, Paulo Freire, and it is dedicated to his memory, struggle and huge achievement.

Finally, any royalties paid to the author of this book will go to UNICEF (the United Nations Children's Fund).

C.S.

INTRODUCTION

Some of the pupils who helped raise £60 by staging a fashion show

Pupils to rescue

WHEN pupils at Earl Marshal School heard some of their friends faced having their free school meals axed, they decided to take action.

A fashion show was arranged and £60 raised for a new fund designed to make sure no one goes hungry.

Around 80 pupils could be hit as part of new regulations proposed under the Government's new Asylum Bill.

Refugees refused citizenship could have benefits and free meals stopped while they wait for appeals to be heard.

Somali and Yemeni pupils at Earl Marshal are expected to be particularly badly hit.

Changes in the system could be introduced as early as the new year.

"The fashion show was a spontaneous expression of concern for their friends and their families," said headteacher Chris Searle.

"Everything was organised by the students, from the catwalk and the clothes to the tickets, posters and music. It was a tremendous effort," he added.

Picture by courtesy of Sheffield Newspapers Ltd

This book takes as its premise that as words are the forerunners and prompters of action, then the teaching of words cannot be separated from encouragement to action.

What manner of words, what manner of action? As a boy, I was schooled during the fag-end days of British imperialism. The Suez Canal was 'taken from us' by Nasser in 1956 when I was in my first year of secondary-modern school, and dozens of African and Caribbean colonies took independence in the years that followed. Yet the inheritance of Empire was still strong, the red stuck out on world atlases we used at school, the children's fiction in the school library glorified imperialism and the words of Lord Meath, the founder of 'Empire Day' were still thematic: that the British must still prove to be 'a Spartan-like, virile race . . . worthy to bear the white man's burden and not be afraid'. I sat in the back pews and watched the Union Jack and flag of St George paraded up the aisle on a Sunday morning, and like millions of others, was there to be persuaded of the 'strong and lofty imperialism which seeks to realise in the British Empire righteousness, peace and joy, which are fundamental principles of the Kingdom of God'.[1]

In this sense I was one of 'Britannia's children', though possibly the last generation to be truly so, acculturated and educated with textbooks, periodicals and Biggles-type fiction (not to mention the public school world of Billy Bunter and 'Hurree Jamset Ram Singh'). I was given 'a version of how to relate to the imperial world and the peoples who lived within it', with, as Kathryn Castle has demonstrated through her scholarship, 'dominance over the "imperial races" a primary message'.[2]

I mention this because I want to make it clear that young English people like myself *were* systematically acculturated and indoctrinated through our schooling with a certain and highly partial (towards the white races and upper classes) view of the world. Yet efforts that teachers like myself have made over the last quarter-century to undo this, to use words as critical tools towards achieving a more just, unprejudiced and class and race-based view of the world, have been caricatured as 'brainwashing', 'indoctrination' and an attempt to destroy all that is equitable and neutral in the English language, its meanings and uses.

Second, I want to underline the central role of the *imagination* in all the teaching examples that follow. The imagination in teaching is the great motivator, the dimension that stretches the mind, provokes engagement in learning and encourages empathy and human understanding. Its influence has often been diminished and sometimes sought to be removed in English education: the *Stepney Words* contestation described in these pages was but one example. I will give two others from the same school experience, simply to illustrate that it is not simply attitudes to imaginative writing and poetry that the conservative influences in schools seek to excise. Take music, in this case the musical genius of the great American jazz pianist, Thelonious Monk. At the time I was doing battle over *Stepney Words*, the progressive music teacher of the school invited two of Britain's foremost jazz musicians – the drummer John Stevens and the alto saxophonist Trevor Watts – into her classroom to introduce her East End students to jazz. As they responded to poetry they responded to the beauty and innovation of the most lucid and percussive of jazz pianists and were soon playing a very basic version of 'Blue Monk', including notes blown and tapped out which escaped from the music room across to other parts of the school. I heard it: it was a free and poignant sound, not raucous, but clear and compelling. Some teachers complained: that was not what school was for – far too distracting, they asserted, and despite the huge motivation and sheer pleasure that the experience gave to the students, it was never allowed again, for the imagination makes too much noise. Monk was banned, just like *Stepney Words*.

Then there was Pasolini. I encouraged the use of film in my classes, and when I heard that the great Italian film-maker's *Gospel According to St Matthew* was being shown free at a local library, I arranged to take my class. Because I had over the maximum of students allowed for one teacher to supervise, a reluctant science teacher – a fervent and very conservative 'Christian' – came with us. He watched some of the film, but when it came to the scene where the young, anti-capitalist Christ overturns the moneylenders' stalls in the Temple with such energy and indignation, that was enough for him, and he walked out. He complained to the headteacher the next day that I was leading the students away from a Christian curriculum and that was another mark on my card. How dare we allow the imagination into anybody's life, let alone the life of Christ the human or the lives of those 'sinful' East London children? Both these incidents told me that without the untrammelled influence of the imagination, very soon there is no education at all.

My fourth point is about mutuality. I have never taught without learning, and believe that there can be no true teaching without learning. The processes of pedagogy involve huge exchanges of understanding and learning new worlds by the teacher side by side with the student. From Stepney East London to Tobago and Grenada in the Caribbean, from Nampula in Mozambique to the 100 per cent working-class Fir Vale in Sheffield, my students and their communities have always been my teachers. In my first published work on language, I wrote as a dedication 'To the children of Tobago, who began my education'. I now understand that somewhere within the spirit of those words is the truest thing I have ever written. For all those places mentioned above and a million others are their own universities, the human beings that live within them their own griots, repositories and scholars. After I left my final school post in Sheffield, I was lucky enough to be employed by Cambridge University. As I walked around that city of scholarly walls, eminent and beautiful buildings and a population of teachers, professors and researchers, I thought 'Yes, there is much to learn here, and much to study'. But I knew there was more in the university of Fir Vale; that within every inner city neighbourhood there is a world to be learned and valued, a microcosm to be understood and all its millions of lessons and narratives to be applied across all avenues of life. And that microcosm shone in the brain of all my ex-students and their parents and grandparents, and it was there to be learned in the shared struggle for human understanding and change.

In this book I have tried to take a longitudinal view: to look back at the responses to the various classroom initiatives of critical literacy with which

I have been involved, the collections of students' work that I have published and the books that I have written on 'English' teaching. These have often been greeted with vituperation and passionate opposition by the lords of education, as if to encourage a critical or alternative view in 'English' lessons in English schools is the worst of all crimes. I have always taught working-class and black students, either in the British inner city, the Caribbean or Africa. My perspectives have been formed through that experience and a working commitment towards those communities, and a wish, with them, to see their children prosper and take power in the world which is theirs. Thus this book is partly an explication of the classroom approaches and the means I have used as a teacher to motivate my students to write, learn and seek to understand the word and the world – but it is also my answer to the criticisms made of those means for over a quarter of a century. It is, of course, a small enough part of a collective attempt to seize back the initiative after many years of conservative restoration in Britain and its schools, but also a continuation of a tradition forged by many teachers over many generations and all continents from the Chartists to the children of Barbiana and Soweto, from the Burston School strikers to Makarenko, Paulo Freire and the pioneers of literacy processes all over the world.

It is dedicated to students and colleagues past in three continents, and the word-work and struggles which they continue to pursue.

Chris Searle, 1998

Notes

1 See David H. Hume, 'Empire Day in Ireland: 1896–1962', in Keith Jeffery (ed.) *An Irish Empire?*, Manchester University Press, 1996.
2 Kathryn Castle, *Britannia's Children*, Manchester University Press, 1996.

1

PRINCIPLES

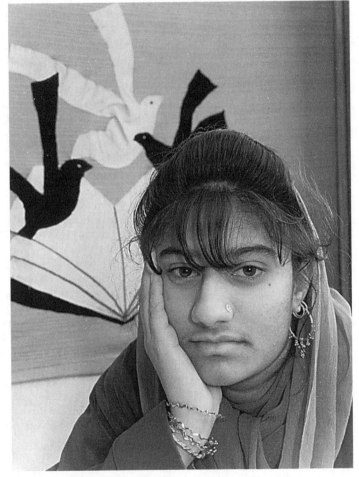

Photograph by courtesy of Sheffield Newspapers Ltd

Towards the end of my first year of teaching in the English school system at an East London comprehensive school, I found myself faced with 800 of my students who had come out on strike. They had written some poems. I had published them locally and then been sacked because the authorities of the school had not liked them. The strike was the students' answer to having their work demeaned in this way. They demonstrated and sang in Stepney churchyard and on the waste ground outside the school gates in the pouring rain, brought other local schools out too in solidarity action, and marched from Stepney to Westminster, rallying again in Trafalgar Square and marching on to Downing Street in an attempt to bring their protest to the prime minister.

Those events proved to be a massive learning experience for me. I had been brought up to accept poetry and literature generally as a part of the English 'canon', sealed away from real life and its emotions; there to be read and studied as classical texts, but not lived and emulated, certainly not to be the cause of strikes and marches. 'Poetry makes nothing happen',[1] W.H. Auden had written (and he was as modern a poet as had been admitted onto our university course); it only 'survives in the valley of its saying', but goes no further. The teenage poets of *Stepney Words* and their schoolmates had refused to accept that and had certainly made something happen, both for me and themselves. Through their action, support, and the publicity that it generated, I regained my job after a long legal battle. It was poetry that had provoked their cultural and collective action, with the strong support of parents, school cleaners and other local people, but primarily through their own intervention. These children of a multiracial working-class community had caused words to become actions.

I shall return to these events and their causes later in these pages, but for me as a teacher they had demonstrated upon my very pulses that the teaching and practice of language and poetry were anything but passive or detached pursuits, and when I went beyond the A level and university 'literature' curricula and read the writing of ordinary East Londoners that had emerged from the titanic struggles of labour over the previous century – the poetry and prose of dockers, matchgirls, tailors, gasworkers, Jews, Irish and Caribbean immigrants, Bangladeshis, Maltese and workers from China and Africa – I realized that there was another tradition of poetry allied to the lives and movement of working-class people that proved the antithesis of Auden's negative words.[2] I sat for hours in the local history room of Mile End library reading the literature proudly published in the *Women's Dreadnaught*, in *Lansbury's Labour Weekly*, in the *East End News* and in the mass of trade union and strike journals and bulletins, in self-published or locally-published collections of poetry and fiction, that gave the heartbeat of the struggling communities not only of the past, but of the one which surrounded me beyond the library walls. I found a whole new literacy, a new curriculum of poetry and life embracing each other for the betterment of those whom it served, and I was determined to make this noble and purposeful use of language and the imagination the centre of any 'English' teaching in my classroom.

For here were words which truly reflected the world but just as truly were determined to transform it for the benefit of those who had the worst of it – whether in the close streets of East London or in the fields of India, the other cities of Europe, the villages of Africa or anywhere in the world where people struggled to better their lives. Words were there as their friends and allies, fused by an imaginative and cultural energy which caused them to combust into action. This sense of the explosive dynamism of language was reinforced in me during the two years that I worked as a secondary-school teacher in Mozambique (from 1976 to 1978).[3] Newly free from Portuguese colonialism after a long armed struggle, the new nation and its liberators looked towards language and literacy as elements of the new armoury of change and development that would propel their new nation out of centuries of poverty, naked exploitation and imperial rule. One of its ministers (for almost all the Mozambique Liberation Front cadres wrote poems as a way of setting down their vision and hope) expressed the power of the people's language in these lines:

> I will forge simple words
> which even the children can understand
> words which will enter every house
> like the wind
> and fall like red hot embers
> on our people's souls.
>
> In our land
> Bullets are beginning to flower.
>
> *Jorge Rebelo*[4]

In the face of such experiences I could no longer see literacy or language itself as neutral or passive areas of learning. Neither could I uphold a pedagogy which stood outside of the struggle of downtrodden people, and allowed events both inside and outside of the classroom to take an unchallenged or unaltered course. Whether it was revolutionary Africa or East London, the direction of language teaching seemed to invoke the same imperative that language must be developed and used as an imaginative tool for the betterment of the lives of those who learned to use it, that the word served the world and those who struggled from below to make it theirs and their children's. Blessed were these wordmakers, for together in language and action they would change and share the Earth.

Language and action: for my teaching the two became inseparable. Literacy was there to understand the world, then change it. It was a message confirmed for me in the writings of Paulo Freire, the Brazlilian literacy teacher who in his books such as *Pedagogy of the Oppressed, Cultural Action for Freedom, Education: The Practice of Freedom* and *Reading the Word and the World*, codified and systematized the insights which I, and many other teachers, had learned through experiences in classrooms across the world. When I read his sentences like 'There is no true word that is not at the same time a praxis. Thus to speak a true word is to transform the world',[5] or encountered such descriptions of students as 'subjects who meet to *name* the world in order to transform it', I experienced the true shock of a teacher's recognition, almost of *déjà vu*. These simply-stated processes were those for which I had striven and to which I aspired: language and its teaching, the imagination and cultural action as one.

Yet Freire's work had been written for those 'out there' and applied in campaigns of literature in Brazil, in Guiné-Bissau, and later in Nicaragua and Grenada. The notion of 'literacy teaching' itself was a process alien to the education system in England, still moulded into a notion of 'English teaching'. It was as foreign as the persona of the poet being 'the leader of the attack'; so strong in the liberation movements and articulated in those words by the Vietnamese leader, Ho Chi Minh. Yet Freire's ideas and teaching processes were anything but irrelevant or romantic, wedded as they were to the real world of 'situational' pedagogy: a literacy forged around real problems to be solved, from the building of latrines to the irrigation of parched fields, from the boiling of water to prevent diarrhoea to an assertion of the rights of women and children and the construction of a sustaining, proud and revolutionary nationhood – all spelled out in the new words and grammar of a liberating literacy.

If such priorities, and the huge energy and release of dialect at the centre of the language eruption in Grenada during the years of the 'Revo' from 1979–83, seemed irrelevant to the European metropoles, the truth was very different.[6] Here was an island full of poets, of the young and old using their own language with a new-found confidence and social legitimacy, while having more opportunity to learn the standard language of the old colonizing power than ever before. When Ernesto Cardenal, the Nicaraguan poet, said of the Grenada Revolution that 'here was the imagination in power',[7] he crystallized the vibrancy, figurative strength and sense of language pride at the centre of the transformations of the island. Language was vehicle and symbol, message and messenger, carrying change yet expressing the heart of that change itself. '*The imagination in power*': now that was what I wanted for all my students.

Being immersed in such a process was the most useful possible re-apprenticeship to teaching again in the British inner city. The multilingual carnival of dialect and mother tongue; the huge interchange of words, images and sounds; the uncertainties and non-comprehension that fed racism; the counter-force of comradeship across a host of languages and cultures; and the placement side by side of differing millions in the inner city neighbourhoods of London, Birmingham, Bradford, Leeds, Liverpool, Manchester and Sheffield – all this fed the possibilities of new approaches to the teaching of literacy that were suddenly calling out for the insights of Freire and the pedagogic dialogues and constructs of 'critical literacy'. The old, conservative and single-tracked approaches to 'English teaching' and 'teaching, reading and writing' were now anachronisms, and ineffectual anachronisms at that. Other pedagogies were imperative to face the new literacies and changing language realities that now surrounded teachers in their daily classroom tasks.

Yet more and more in the 1980s and 1990s in English schools, necessary new pedagogies were being blocked and repudiated by the force of conservative restoration, the new barbarism of a market system of education and the curriculum hegemony being imposed across all British state schools, through the uniformity and 'orders' of a command curriculum – the 'National Curriculum'.[8] This was a narrow, racist, state-licensed and pre-cooked version of classroom 'delivery' rather than true classroom dialogue and creation, and became the fulfilment of the worst fears of William Blake, the London poet, where 'in a desolate market . . . they enclosed my infinite brain into a narrow circle'[9].

The development of a dialogue-based pedagogy and critical literacy is not an easy task in such a system where all is to be prescribed, outcomes are to be preordained, examined by ceaseless testing and overseen by OFSTED (Office for Standards in Education), the new schools inspectorate and curriculum police. The obstructions and permanent surveillance are formidable and offer little space for democratic practice and creative sharing of knowledge and experience between student and teacher – the foundation of a truly progressive pedagogy. Then, beyond the curriculum confines of school, there is the 'predatory culture' of post-industrial capitalism in which an entire generation of young people are threatened to become immersed. As described by McLaren, this culture is one of 'image-value' rather than the imagination, trans-nationalism rather than internationalism, filled by 'a stark obsession with power fed by the voraciousness of capitalism's global voyage'. Predatory culture is the great deceiver. It marks 'the ascendancy of the dehydrated imagination that has lost its capacity to dream otherwise' from virtual realities and corrosive games of violence, egotism, copy-cat imitation and cyber-clouds of death-fantasy.[10] It is the opposite of life, generosity, empathy and people's solidarity. It subsumes the truly human and projects a new barbarism which threatens to smother social life and the very bonds that keep us capable of being one human race.

Such are the enemies of critical literacy and creative pedagogy, and such is the struggle facing teachers and students in classrooms at the turn of this millenium. In this context only the polar opposite to this culture of savagery will suffice. Education needs to be revolutionary in human conception in order to contest it. We are back to Freire and a process of educating that involves dialogue, reflection and action that is 'really *human*, empathetic, loving, communicating and humble, in order to be liberating'.[11] It is in the spirit of these words that I have attempted to write and compile this book, itself a reflection of pedagogy and classroom examples developed over a quarter-century of teaching and learning with school students from British inner cities, in particular from those in the East Ends of London and Sheffield. These are examples, not exemplars, for they need to be considered critically and read as attempts which made both success and failure in varying degrees, but which at all times moved my own thinking and practice forward, sometimes consolidating and sometimes subverting previous critical insight.

Certain fundamental stages characterized the process of teaching I adopted, in my objective to move my students through the activities of critical literacy and creative writing. For simplicity's sake and by way of creating a mnemonic, I have identified each stage with one of eight words, all beginning with the letter 'C': **creation, consideration, consciousness, confidence, collaboration, consolidation, cultural action** and **crossover**, with the five words following 'creation' frequently changing places and order. In this sequence the creator of a new form of words and language becomes the doer, the person of action, as a result of the new understanding and confidence she or he has gained through inventing new ways of making language in working cooperation with his or her classmates. The act of **creation** involves the mobilization of words and the imagination in response to a certain situation under discussion or dialogue, as Freire put it, a 'reflection upon situationality' – the place, the context, the causes. What is created is some new pattern of language, new poetical thoughts, new configurations of words and images that are forged by an individual, a pairing or a group who are enlarging the situation they are considering, treating it with empathy, applying their imaginations. Such activity and its result in written literature is consolidated by reflection and **consideration** in acts of individual and collective thinking about the new work on the page. This leads to the beginnings of a new **consciousness**, for here are thoughts freshly forged, newly expressed in combinations of words and images previously unimagined and made articulate. This achievement of the literate imagination provokes new levels and energies of **confidence**, both in the creative self and in others who have worked in **collaboration**. It may indeed cause an individual writer to engage in a collaborative project, or **consolidation of** the cooperative work that has already been successfully completed. It is from this confidence in achievement and the added encouragement gained from working on a successful and creative exercise with others, that the determination is engendered for **cultural action** at a later time – as some of the examples in following chapters will clearly show.

Working in a classroom where many languages are at work – be they represented by more than one variety of English, Punjabi, Arabic, Somali, Bengali, Sylheti or various Caribbean Creole vernaculars, and where cultural symbols and narratives are broad and different the **crossover** of culture becomes an emphatic objective of critical pedagogy and literacy development. With the 'imagination in power', cultures and languages are exchanged and shared. Through empathy, the others become oneself and oneself becomes the others, and humanity mobilizes all its sharing of spirit and moment. From such creative crossover comes the exercise of human and cultural solidarity, and a new process of learning through the imagination's real flesh and blood and capacity to *become* other humans in far-flung situations. An example is the white girl Sallie, writing in Sheffield in her poem 'Immortal', about black youth resisting apartheid in the Soweto townships, expressed in 1989 at a particularly intense moment of South-African struggle:

> They'll live forever
> And never die
> They're joined to us
> More often than ever.

> We breathe for them,
> Fight for them,
> Live for them
> We *are* them.[12]

The enormous human shift to *becoming* in the final line is the moment of profound solidarity with other humans. Freire expressed this movingly in *The Pedagogy of the Oppressed*. For it is when the content of teaching and learning 'constantly expands and renews itself'. Another example is the anonymous lines left on a desk by a classmate which I picked up and read after all the students had left that same lesson on South Africa, which show that solidarity moves even further, from thought and reflection to a pledge for action and change. That these lives cannot continue to endure such degradation and human oppression:

> I see blood red as I'm waking
> Thinking,
> Thinking about the way we live.
> Pulsing,
> My blood runs through my veins.
>
> We've got to change it!

At all stages or at any moment of the process of classroom work there is one other 'C' which the teacher must never be reticent to express or add, as a part of her or his basic function as a teacher – the task of **correction**. The teacher shares the learning experience with the students, and will often marvel at the power and originality of their creative effort and achievement. But his or her task is to enlarge that achievement and spark its emulation by ensuring that it is at its best. This means that the teacher is constantly circulating among the students, correcting and extending their punctuation, spelling, grammar, sentence structure, paragraphing – advising on new drafts, fresh or incipient ideas and expression at the point of their development and articulation, assisting and being the catalyst to students working together, or working on the same page of the student who is writing or creating alone.

Critical literacy can only be a credible pedagogy if it extends and enlarges the powers of language of the students and gives them the opportunity and ability to be in full control of all the words they need. This means an understanding of basic grammar and sentence analysis, the power to spell correctly and use punctuation effectively, to know the figures of speech and write sequentially and coolly, as well as with creative strength and full imaginative energy. In short, critical literacy can only become the basis of a genuinely critical and interventionist foundation for life and action if it successfully brings the student into the world of the word in all its forms: written, spoken, poeticized, analytical, cognitive, and affective, and has offered a social and personal language strong and confident enough to challenge, contend and struggle with, and seek and find solutions to, the personal and political problems that face the urban young person at the tip of our century. The process of gradually gaining control of the technical aspects of the standard language while freely expressing the mother tongue, and the building of an armoury of words and an ability to put them in the correct places through a working understanding of the rules of the languages we use, are at the centre of critical literacy and form its basic objective.[13] It is with control of language and words, working under our full jurisdiction, that we begin to see them as change-agents in our experiences of the world, and effective counters against those forces who oppose and threaten our life upon the planet. What I wrote in the introduction to *Classrooms of Resistance*[14] in 1976 I believe still to be true, perhaps, given the pile-up of post-industrial oppression that surrounds as everywhere as late capitalism is exerting its power, even more true than it was then: 'the priority was that these working class children should learn to read, write, spell, punctuate, to develop the word as a weapon and tool in the inevitable struggles for improvement and liberation for them, and the rest of their class all over the world'.

Unless 'critical literacy' pursues and achieves such concrete, real and visceral objectives, it means nothing, it stays a slogan, neither offering the ability to read and write or the rationale to analyse, reflect and act, and by doing so, change for the better the world of learners and teachers everywhere, starting from the little worlds within and around their schools. For unless, as Freire epitomized it in *Education: The Practice of Freedom*, 'critical understanding leads to critical action',[15] it remains an exercise and never a real intervention. And fused with the critical is the creative. They become inseparable, mutually life-enhancing and meaning-enhancing – and the antithesis of the dead hand of prescribed or 'national' curricula, in the forging of a teaching method and a democratic classroom scholarship which would 'itself be an act of creation, capable of releasing other creative acts'.

Critical literacy is solid, real, immediate – a learning and living tool which breaks open the word and the world for the learner. It is the process of teaching and learning the achievement of language, put to the use of the creative understanding of the world, and the human struggle for its betterment through cultural action. As the literacy scholar Colin Lankshear wrote in a review of *School of the World*, it embodies 'a pedagogy which wilfully harnesses the task of learning to be literate in English to the larger ends of practising in deeds as well as words the moral and civic art of living justly and democratically'.[16] That is the interpretation that this book pursues, and that is the objective of this particular teacher. In the following pages I hope we can meet, agree and disagree, but move our words and those of our students further forward: all our words.

Notes

1 W.H. Auden, 'In Memory of W.B. Yeats' from *Selected Poems of W.H. Auden*, Faber and Faber, London, 1979.
2 See Chris Searle (ed.), *Bricklight: Poems of the Labour Movement in East London*, Pluto Press, London, 1980.

3 Chris Searle, *We're Building the New School! Diary of a Teacher in Mozambique*, 2ed Press, London, 1980.
4 Jorge Rebelo, 'Come, Brother, and Tell Me Your Life', quoted in Chris Searle (ed.) *Sunflower of Hope: Poems from the Mozambican Revolution*, Allison and Busby, London, 1980.
5 Paulo Freire, *The Pedagogy of the Oppressed*, Penguin, London, 1972.
6 Chris Searle, *Words Unchained: Language and Revolution in Grenada*, 2ed Press, London, 1984.
7 Chris Searle, *Grenada Morning: A memoir of the Revo*, Karia Press, London, 1990.
8 See Chris Searle, *Living Community, Living School*, Tufnell Press, London, 1997.
9 See Peter Ackroyd, *Blake*, Sinclair-Stevenson, London, 1996.
10 Peter McLaren, *Critical Pedagogy and Predatory Culture*, Routledge, London, 1995.
11 Paulo Freire, op. cit.
12 Chris Searle (ed.), *Freedom Children: A Tribute in Poetry to the Young People of South Africa from the Young People of Sheffield*, Sheffield City Council, Sheffield, 1990.
13 See Chris Searle, 'A Common Language', in, *Race and Class*, 25 (2), 1983.
14 Chris Searle: Classrooms of Resistance: Writers and Readers Cooperative, London, 1976.
15 Paulo Freire, *Education: the Practice of Freedom*, Writers and Readers Cooperative, London, 1975.
16 Colin Lankshear, review of 'School of the World', *Race and Class*, 37 (4), 1996.

2

STEPNEY WORDS

Ramona, Pauline and Stepney Words. Photograph © The Times

When I came to teach 'English' at a secondary school in Stepney, East London in 1970, two major themes preoccupied me. One was that within spoken 'English' there were hundreds of non-standard, dialectal versions of the language that held a volcanic power of figurative and assertive speech that I known first from the 'common' speech of English working-class speakers from all parts of the country, and second from the language of the Eastern Caribbean, where I had begun my career as a schoolteacher of English in the late 1960s.[1] The second theme involved a particular interest in teaching poetry and creative writing. This was something I had begun to develop while teaching in Tobago, but a year studying 'English in education' at Exeter University with a powerful tutor called Marjorie Hourd, also influenced me decisively. At that time she was into her seventies, but still a teacher of enormous dynamism.

In her books *The Education of the Poetic Spirit* and *Coming into their Own*, Hourd argued strongly for the writing of poetry in the classroom as an energy for developing both the confidence and understanding of individual children and the strength of the union between them 'as a means of binding people together at the point where they are most truly themselves'.[2] She argued too for the centrality of a 'knitting together of thought and feeling', given that 'a large population of the stuff which children learn at school is dead wood', and that 'vital parts of knowledge are sifted out and brought into contact with the increased degree of vividness' which a child experiences. Long before I read of notions of 'critical literacy' I had encountered a similar concept in the work of Hourd, who wrote in *Coming into their Own*: 'So subtle and incalculable is the outcome of any reason where the *creative-critical* principle is at work, that a teacher cannot always expect to succeed' (my emphasis).

Armed with such insights and constraints, I was determined to pursue this 'creative-critical principle' into my own teaching. I was also determined to teach in East London. While at university in Leeds and Canada I had grown into poetry through the words of Isaac Rosenberg, the Jewish Stepney poet who had been killed during the last days of the 1914–18 war. I had written my Master's thesis on his poetry and longed to share his world – the streets where he had wandered as a young man which had grounded his startling poetic vision and use of language. These streets of Tower Hamlets also formed the closest inner city neighbourhoods to my own greater London and Essex boyhood haunts of Romford and Hornchurch. But in terms of the structures and anachronisms of the school in which I found myself working, I probably could not have found a less promising situation had I tried with all my efforts. Sir John Cass and Red Coat School in Stepney, East London, was a Church of England foundation school established in 1710 and named after a City of London merchant and alderman who was its founder. Divided into 'guilds' as a substitute for the public school structure of houses, and led by 'guild wardens', rigidly streamed from an 'A' to a 'remedial' class of over 30 inmates, it was frequently patrolled by a particular 'deputy guild warden', an anglican priest who wandered the corridors in academic gown, clerical collar and unsheathed cane, searching for 'rebrobate' pupils. Although in name of genre a 'comprehensive' school, it seemed to have missed out on decades of educational progress and was in a time-warp of its own. Every year on 'Founder's Day' the school students were marched to Aldgate Church for a service of remembrance to the founder, and given red feathers to wear – thus commemorating the moment of Sir John Cass' death, when he coughed up blood over the quill he was using to sign his will, which gave a part of his wealth for the maintenance of the school.

But what soon became very clear to me was the contradiction between the repressive and absurd framework of the school itself, and the huge vitality of its working-class students and the language that they spoke, and, if encouraged, the words they could write. Filled with the stimulation of the creative work of my ex-students in the Caribbean and the teaching both of Marjorie Hourd and my old school English teacher, Norman Hidden – a poet and publisher of *Workshop*, a national poetry journal – I embarked upon a pedagogy based upon creative writing, particularly poetry, in my 'English' lessons. I asked the students to look at the world immediately around them in East London, and the people in the streets, houses and council estates close to the school. Remembering Blake and his assertion that 'the streets are my ideas for my imagination', I took my classes for walks along the streets and to the parks, squares and churchyards of Stepney, getting them to bring their exercise books for observations, images and draft lines that they could later incorporate into descriptions and poems. They noticed in particular old people, the unemployed, mothers and their children, people at work and the homeless, many of whom were schizophrenics. These were people they saw every day, but now they were being asked to look at them in new ways, to invent metaphors and similes, to see them more closely as the source of language and a subject of empathy. They also looked around the school at their classmates and teachers, at their faces and into their minds, and one student saw that:

> My classroom is dim and dull
> My teacher sits there thinking
>
> She's so dim and dull
> That she just sits there thinking
>
> The world is dim and dull
> My life is not worth living[3]

Exploring with their imaginations the loneliness of the aged, the marginalized and alienated, they found the same feelings in themselves and wrote in the simplest and most poignant of words:

> I am old and frightened
> in this darkened world
> I'm shut behind bars . . .
>
> *Margaret*

I live on my own
Have no friends
It's damp and dark
I've got voices in my ears
But they're all in my mind

Margaret

or:

I live on my own
In a cold damp room
No one to talk to
No one to see

My children are married
They live far away
My husband died
On a cold winter's day

Tina

This language, which Professor James Britton of Goldsmiths College, University of London, called ' "unliterary" but full of honesty and conviction',[4] ranged from the powerful and rebelliously familiar energy of dialect and slang:

I come from Stepney, lived here all me life
Loads of cheap markets
Bargains at half price
Jumpers and skirts, trousers cheap
All muddled up in any old heap

Dirty old women, shouting out their wares,
Everybody stinks, nobody cares
All dirty, greasy things bunged into bins,
Stinkin' rotten hole is Stepney

Diane

to the affectionate, almost chorus-like:

I think Stepney is a very smokey place
But I like it
People in Stepney do things wrong
But I like them
Everything in Stepney has its disadvantages
But I like it

It does not have clean air like the country
But I like it

The buildings are old and cold
But I like them
The summer is not very hot
But I like it

Rosemary

The visits to the local churchyard across the road from the school produced some poems most tender and gentle:

Autumn Morning in Stepney Churchyard

The church was standing in a spot where the light of
    a thousand candles was glowing in the mist of the
    morning
And the faint beams of sunlight came through, and
    the cold air was gently overflowing and in a second
    it was gone
The churchyard was dead and the birds only were there
And the leaves were falling,
                    falling,
                            falling,
And the dew that lay by the ever-lay leaves is fainting
        into the background to die.

Lesley

I marvelled at her use of imagery – and where did she find the 'ever-lay leaves'? All the formal learning of 'figures of speech', all that 'onomatopoeia' and 'assonance' – it all melted when I read these lines. For here it was manifested by an 11-year-old poet whose language of surprise sprang into life and beauty.

The *Times Educational Supplement* likened *Stepney Words* to 'a commentary on Blake. These are the real children of Albion',[5] its reviewer, Richard Burns, wrote. And remembering Blake's 'The Garden of Love', Karen's poem of Stepney Churchyard echoed the sensitivity of the greatest of London's poets. I wondered, had she ever read:

So I turn'd to the Garden of Love
That so many sweet flowers bore;

And I saw that it is filled with graves
And tombstones where flowers should be . . .

(Blake *The Garden of Love*)

Karen's words were these:

The grass is covered by brown leaves
The sun is pouring through the trees
The dew on the grass is delicate
Like a baby's tear.
The grass mingles with the graves

Behind the graves there dwells fear
The church is ancient with its dull-coloured walls
Surrounded by black railings
Surrounded by trees
All ancient
So I'm sitting on a bench as the sun goes down
Night draws in, all goes calm.

And I believed that only the special knowing and empathy of a child's vision of the world could have invented the image of dew 'like a baby's tear'.

One day, in the middle of my marking and typing up of these poems, I visited an exhibition of local photographs at Whitechapel Library by a young photographer from Liverpool, Ron McCormick. In the photographs I found the same local world as that represented in the poems – images of East London people that projected the same resonance, empathy and the artist's eagerness to enter the lives of his subjects, portrayed with a vividness, simplicity and sense of discovery. I left a note in the visitors' book, suggesting that Ron McCormick and I should meet and discuss these similarities between his images and my students' words. The photographer called at my flat the next day. We began a working friendship that was to last many years. He took copies of some of the poems and superimposed their words across poster-size blow-ups of photographs which seemed to be making similar statements – pictures of old people, a boy kicking a football across a stretch of waste ground, a young Asian girl photographed against a brick and rubble wall. A few weeks later he brought these enlarged images into my English class, and we used them as a stimulus for further poems and creative writing, prompting the students to identify with their subjects and imagine their lives and realities. I did not know it at the time, for at that point I had never read the work of Paulo Freire and his literacy teaching in Recife in north-eastern Brazil, but what we were doing was very much akin to the use made by Freire of 'situation' images in the 'culture circles' of the urbanized peasants he taught, and as described in *Education: The Practice of Freedom*.[6] The difference was that we were using the grain of photographic images rather than the lines of Freire's sketches, and we had the dimension of the students' creative efforts as a further impetus towards encouraging their classmates to emulate their achievements. Freire had written in *Literacy: Reading the Word and the World* of the need to start critical literacy development from the 'word universe' of the students. Here, in Stepney, was just such a localized world, a universe of sensations, felt by a group of students having about them a vibrant internationalism. With their origins in Bengal, Ghana, Gibraltar, Cyprus and Jamaica among many other countries, they were now, collectively, in the immediate cosmos of the East London streets. The local was meeting the global, fused together by the spirit of the history and struggles of the world, and all this was taking place in the immediate neighbourhood. 'Education is an act of love, and thus an act of courage', Freire had written. 'It cannot fear the analysis of reality.' These classroom sessions with Ron came bounding back in my memory years later when I read of Freire's talk at York University during a visit to Britain in 1976, and later read his books. 'We do not work in the air, but in a concrete way in the structure of society', he had declared.[7]

Yet it was that very 'concrete' aspect of the Stepney children's poetry that began to cause perturbation among those who controlled the school. Ron and I assembled a number of the poems, juxtaposed with the photographs, and suggested to the headteacher that the school might want to finance an anthology. He seemed interested, but said he needed to discuss the idea with the school governors, who were composed, in the main, of city businessmen, clerics and a local councillor, with an ex-colonial High Court judge (also a City parish priest) as vice-chair and the local vicar as chair. The young poets' conception of the real and concrete world around them on all sides did not fit with these 'governors' view of the world, and they objected to what they declared was an 'unbalanced', 'gloomy', and 'drab' vision being expressed in the anthology, and signalled their disapproval of the themes of its poetry. 'Was there not other material of a more cheerful character?'[8] asked the chair, indicating that the governors themselves wished to reconstruct the anthology giving it a much more 'cheerful cockney sparrow' theme, rather than focusing on the real world and the solid social view that the students were exploring.

Meanwhile, Ron and myself had worked to gain local support for the draft anthology – which we had called *Stepney Words* – and secured interest and financial contributions for its publication from a number of people living locally. We had visited many of the poets' parents, as well as helpful individuals whom we thought could help us find the money to produce the collection as a community booklet. We found tremendous encouragement and financial help from a local plumber, a librarian, a social worker and two other very influential individuals in particular, who were very moved by the students' work. One was Jack Dash, the retired dockers' leader, a communist and trade unionist who was also the chair of the Tenants Association of the Mount Morres council estate, which backed on to the school. Dash, a man of enormous creative dynamism, was a devoted reader and lover of poetry. A humorist too, he wrote his own epitaph as a rhyme:

> Here lies Jack Dash
> All he wanted was
> To separate them from their cash

He ended his autobiography *Good Morning Brothers!*[9] by quoting four lines that seemed to give a grounding hope and reason for our work too:

> Ah Love! could thou and I with fate conspire
> To grasp this sorry Scheme of Things entire,
> Would we not shatter it to bits – and then
> Re-mould it nearer to the Heart's Desire!

Jack Dash was a great enthusiast for the idea of the poetry collection, as was the Bishop of Stepney, Father Trevor Huddleston, who lived a few houses along Commercial Road from me. Huddleston was the ex-Anglican priest of Sophiatown, a black neighbourhood near Johannesburg, in South Africa, and was a friend of Mandela and the stalwarts of the African National Congress. He had spoken out, worked and compaigned tirelessly against apartheid for many years until he was recalled in 1956 by his order, the Community of the Resurrection. His book of the same year *Naught for Your Comfort*,[10] which exposed the racist rule in South Africa, had sold 250,000 copies. He had become the Bishop of Masasi in Tanzania and had then returned to this East London diocese. Perhaps his identification with the *Stepney Words* poems arose from his understanding, expressed in a pamphlet for the National Union of Teachers in 1969, that 'Loneliness and isolation appear to be the most characteristic features of life in the modern secular cities of the world', and his view that 'what is most desperately needed is an enlargement of imagination'.[11] When Ron McCormick and I showed him the poems, he was overwhelmed by them and immediately offered to give us as much help as he could to enable them to reach published form.

With such committed support, and the financial contributions from neighbours, parents and some teachers at the school, we decided to go ahead with the anthology as a community publication. The disapproval of the governors only made us more determined to see that the poems were published. From a small Jewish printshop in Brick Lane, *Stepney Words* emerged in early April 1971. By the end of the month all the poets had their own free copies and the poetry had been reprinted in the local and national press, in feature articles in the *Daily Mirror*, the *Daily Sketch* (its final issue), the *Sun* and the *East London Advertiser*, and I had been given notice by the governors for (as the local education authority divisional officer put it) 'flagrant disobedience and the refusal to obey the orders of a superior officer', or as the chair of governors expressed it, the first and greatest sin of 'spiritual pride' – all for the publication of the 32 pages of *Stepney Words*.

We had sent copies to educationists and reviewers all over the country, as well as to local teachers and poets whom we thought would be interested. But it was primarily a 'community communication', as we categorized it, and it was widely distributed all over East London, with free copies put in doctors' waiting rooms, community centres, libraries and anywhere we thought people would go and have time to read. We had many letters of appreciation and support: from A.S. Neill of 'Summerhill', and from Sir Alec Clegg, the pioneering and reforming chief education officer of the West Riding of Yorkshire, who later wrote in the *Times Educational Supplement*[12] that 'it so moved me by its depth of feeling and by the statement that it made as a whole that I took what was for me, after 26 years in Yorkshire, the wholly unprecedented step of sending a modest contribution towards the next issue'. Clegg added that he hoped that my dismissal would not deter 'other teachers from encouraging this kind of writing or from inducing children to show a critical concern for the circumstances of the community in which they live'. Poets too, gave their support, recognizing the function of the children's work, as well as its beauty. D.J. Enright, a poet whose work I had studied in my own sixth-form schooldays, wrote in *Encounter*: 'But what is inescapably painful, and frightening, about these laconic verses, and finally most impressive, is the children's clearsightedness, their unwavering gaze – or, at any rate, the total absence of illusion'.[13]

This direct and non-illusory quality of the language coming from these young Stepney poets was vividly expressed in a poem called 'Facts and Fantasy' by 15 year old Sandra, in the midst of her GCSE examination class.

> Fantasy is so unreal
> but it's nice to dream
> Fact puts the truth to you
> so it's quite cruel.
>
> People escape to fields of fantasy
> because they can't face the truth,
> but, never mind, the time will come
> for them to see the facts.
>
> Life flies past in a world of fantasy,
> but in fact it goes quite slow,
> so why dream of fantasy
> when you have to see the truth some day.

It reflected 11 year old Timmy's imaginative musings from the womb: what was this gamble to be lived? It was Blake again, and *Infant Sorrow*:

The Chance

> Here I am lonely in my mother's womb
> As I am lying here, I am wondering
> just whether to come out and see the bright world.
> But maybe it's not a bright world.
> It's maybe dull, but I can't tell if it is a dull world.
> I will not be able to get back into the womb if it is dull.
> It is just a chance I will have to take.

The same 'unwavering gaze' that Enright described was a profoundly moral lens that focused upon these poets' rejection of the illusions of a drugs-based escapism. The nakedness of their words reached inside the agony of the teenager Gale – homeless, imprisoned, addicted – in the television film *Gale is Dead* which they watched and wrote about:

> Gale is dead
> we shed a tear
> Nobody knew what she wanted.
> She wanted a mother . . .

For 'up west' were more things than money, clothes, glamour and clubs. There was also Piccadilly, painted in the simple, but relentness words and truth from these East London children: language without avoidance, without lies, sweeping down with Lorraine's poem in a cadence of the real world:

> Along the streets of the Dilly
> people are sitting close together,
> trying to find an escape from life . . .
>
> But their world is seen in a haze of dreams
> It would never, never be true.
> But once you've had to escape once
> you will have to escape over
> > over
> > over
> > again.

Adrian Mitchell, the socialist poet, recognized the pedagogical thinking behind *Stepney Words*, and in an article vindicating poetry itself in the *Sunday Times*[14] asserted that 'the aim must be the very immodest one of destroying the causes of deprivation by exposing them and explaining them to the children themselves. These are the kids who have the greatest need for poetry – their own poetry'. The author of *English For The Rejected* and other seminal books on English teaching, David Holbrook, compared the poems of *Stepney Words* to the writing of Yeats, Solzhenitsyn, Shakespeare, James Baldwin, Seamus Heaney and Arthur Waley's translations of Chinese poetry, saying: 'they speak of the human predicament at its deepest level of suffering and aspiration', affirming their 'skill and deep existentialist passion' and declaring that 'for children to be trained to mean what they say is a great gift to their humanity – not least in a world which is so full of the trivial, superficial and meretricious'.[15] Yet all these critical compliments were but noises off to the students themselves. Their own 'cultural action' was confirmed on the green outside the school, next to the churchyard where many of them had composed their poems. Eight-hundred students – virtually the entire school, came out on strike and rallied against the sacking of a teacher who had published their poems. Even as they boycotted class they sang and proclaimed poems. They held aloft a banner with their own poem in support of their sacked teacher and sang an old music-hall song, 'Roll out the Barrel', punning on the name of the headteacher, Geoffrey Barrell. In 1996, some 25 years after these events, one of the strikers – Tony Harcup, now a professional journalist – wrote about them in the *New Statesman*:[16]

I was 14 and in the third year at the time. I recall two fifth-form girls coming into our classroom one afternoon to announce that Searle had been sacked for publishing the booklet. There was to be a mass meeting after school on the green opposite. Hundreds of us turned up, some merely curious but most outraged that the school should sack a teacher who had introduced us to drama and creative writing (the Mersey Poets and all that), who had given up his evenings to run a school film club, who actually lived locally and treated us with respect.

As one parent commented: 'He's the only teacher who lives here in the slums and tries to understand the children.'

We voted to strike the next day. Secret ballots had not been heard of in those days, so we voted docker-style as seen on T.V., by a show of hands. The following morning I saw hundreds of pupils on the green, and none in the playground. The bell went, but 800 of us stayed outside all morning, singing, chanting and waving our ties above our heads as a string of teachers urged us to go in. Some were sympathetic, others hostile, but we ignored them all, staying out in the rain as first the police and then the media turned up to see what the fuss was all about.

After several hours, a delegation of strikers was allowed in to hold fruitless talks with the Head. The next day about 200 pupils returned to school, to be denounced as 'scabs' by the majority who had quickly learnt the language of pre-Thatcher industrial relations.

Several hundred of us marched from Stepney to Trafalgar Square that day. 'Young militants on the march' was the headline in the *Evening Standard*. Our action was covered on T.V. and in the papers, and pupils at Stepney Green and other nearby schools were quick to take secondary action to support us.

At the neighbouring Stepney Green School the students were locked in by orders of their headteacher, but scores climbed the tall brick walls to join the Sir John Cass strikers. Two 14-year-old girls wrote their own narrative poem describing the strike. They wrote of the:

> Weeks of preparation for our
> Writing to be in print.
> Our big chance came for
> Something that we could call our own.
> And finally the book was published and sold.
> Everybody liked it, it had the truth in it,
> But the governors did not like it.

And later:

> These were no longer children,
> These were people sticking up for their rights.
> The school was painted
> Wall to wall
> Begging them to bring Chris back,
> But we weren't going to beg for long.
>
> Children planned, mothers planned,
> Till finally a decision was made.
> 'Let's strike until he comes back!
> 'Let's sing, let's chant and scream!'
> Everybody was with us,
> Even the cleaners refused to
> > scrub his name from the walls.

Parents too joined the demonstration outside the school gates. They had been mobilized by their sons and daughters, and by the arrogance of the chairman of governors on the first day of the strike. As one mother recalled at a later hearing before the authorities:

During the strike, on one particular day, it was raining and some of the children went into Stepney Church, which is opposite the school, to shelter from the rain. The Vicar, who is Chairman of the Governors, came to them and said: 'Get out of my church you ruffians, get out!' The children found this extremely difficult to understand because very often they attend church services when the church is referred to as 'their' church, and they were unable to reconcile the Vicar's attitude.[17]

The same mother attested during another hearing:

I had to admire the kids for doing it, I really did, because to me it showed that they had taken the grown-ups' part. The grown-ups at the school were acting like children. This to me was the Governors' attitude. They were acting like children. It was as though the kids had taken over the adults' part by going on strike. This is what it seemed to me. If I had not been at work I think I would have been down there with the kids.

Other parents described how writing poetry had motivated their children positively, changed their homework habits, strengthened their confidence to learn and encouraged them to take a great deal more interest in school generally: 'One evening I attended the Tower Hamlets Community Centre and listened to boys of 14 and 15 years old reading their own poems and I found this most moving, especially as normally these boys would be out on the streets, possibly breaking windows etc,' said one mother. She later said of her daughter:

She used to sit at home of an evening and write poetry. She was always good at English but she had never written poetry before. I mean, I thought it was a marvellous idea to publish them because, let us face it, kids in Stepney have not got much of a good outlook and to see their poems published in a book, well, I thought this was abosolutely marvellous. My daughter has lots of friends and I know their parents. We have spoken of it. They were all in favour of it.

Another mother told how her daughter had involved her in the poems that she was writing: 'She used to go upstairs and write, you know. She would come to me and say "What do you think of this?", and well, when I went to school it all had to rhyme, but now apparently it does not have to rhyme – and that is still poetry.' The commitment of the children spread to the parents, and soon the community itself had embraced *Stepney Words* and taken it as *their* book, something worth struggling for that had been made by the work and creativity of their own children.

Support and reaction came from afar. One particular poem provoked a lot of interest and understanding when it was re-published in the *Daily Mirror*. There had been a dustmans' strike in London at the time that *Stepney Words* was being prepared, and 11-year-old Maxine had written this extraordinary poem. As she bagged up her neighbours' rubbish left on the pavements, earning sixpence a bag, suddenly the rubbish became friendly – a source of extra pocket money, and a new way of seeing.

> I, the lonely dustman, go walking along the dusty streets,
>   my only truthful friends are the rubbish.
> They come rushing against me, so that I can throw my
>   only friends away into the world of rubbish.
> Every day my friends are thrown into the streets and put
>   into iron cages,
> And they rely on me to take them out of a dreadful, dirty
>   and awkward world of horror
> Then along comes a different world.
> It's a dust-cart.
> Then once more my friends rush against me and I throw
>   them into a world of darkness.
> But now we are on strike, I see my friends wherever I go.

And from Devon came a letter from a working dustman; he wrote to Maxine's mother:

> I saw Maxine's verse in the *Daily Mirror*, and I think she has a real understanding of people like the dustman and his world of the dustcart, and the bins full of rubbish. As a dustman myself I can see the love and hate that go with the job, up early in the morning in all sorts of weather and thinking who will be my best friend today?
> The dustcart really is a different world, for the people are glad to know you once a week and then forget all about you until the day comes round again. Some say Hello but mostly prefer to keep a safe distance.

Here was a discourse of poetry and the real world across a country, provoked by a child's poem in a London neighbourhood and answered by a reader in a far county of England, whose own working life echoed the words he had read – a true community of the poetic spirit. He ended his letter with these words: 'I think all the verses of the children in the *Mirror* showed understanding of the world they live in, and that what is missing is true friendship between people.'

I could only marvel at such developments, and *Stepney Words* provoked many such moments. For me, the letter I received from my former university teacher at Exeter, the veteran Marjorie Hourd who had prompted my interest in children's poetry, moved me as much as the poems. For to have your own teachers supporting your work, staying with you in their confidence, is a most sustaining and strengthening force. In a letter she sent to me shortly after she had seen television news reports of the strike, she wrote: 'I nearly wept when I saw your kids crossing Trafalgar Square on Friday – I felt that all I have fought for in nearly 40 years was indeed coming to pass'. And my old school English teacher, Norman Hidden, now chairman of the Poetry Society, answered poetry with poetry, writing the following poem and seeing its publication in *Tribune*.[18] He prefaced his 'Protest Verse' with a quotation from a news report of the strike in *The Times*: 'The children on strike stayed outside in the pouring rain. The vicar of a church opposite threatened to call the police when some of them tried to get into the church for shelter'.

Protest Verse

They've sacked Chris Searle today
Anonymous men in clerical grey
Who govern with absolute rule
this voluntary aided
Church of England
ever so Christian school.

It may be joy, it may be misery:
But suffer the children to write what they see,
Quickly the answer came back:
They gave him the sack, the sack, the sack
from this voluntary aided
ever so Christian School.

We'll publish some of the poems, the governors said,
The ones that are 'pretty' – and pretty nigh dead!
The rest of course will never do,
They're far too fresh and much too true
for this voluntary aided
Victorianly faded
C. of E. School.

We cannot say the writing's pornographic
It merely shows the people, the streets, the traffic.
But we'd prefer the bright-eyed vision narrow
into the dead old cliché, 'cheerful cockney sparrow'
In this happy, oh so happy,
Church of England school.

And so they've sacked Chris Searle today
Who broke their first commandment: to obey.
Governors who preach the truth, the life, the way –
Get down on your knees and pray, pray, pray
for your ever so Christian
Tarnished and faded,
Your ever so Christian soul.

For my own part, I was overwhelmed by this support. It created a storm of my own critical literacy, and later I wrote:

> This loyalty from those whom I taught and those who had taught me transformed my understanding of the power of language and the power of poetry. I was beginning to see 'Literature' now as something living, no longer a dead artefact but dynamic, organic, charged with political protest and a cry for justice. For the actions of the children, plus the support of parents, teachers and the National Union of Teachers meant that after a two-year legal struggle I could walk back into the same school and continue the tasks of teaching. So the strike had presaged a victory for teachers such as myself.[19]

The action of the students, their courage and organization, had made the *Stepney Words* affair a national – even international – issue, as friends sent me cuttings from reports in Melbourne, Toronto and Trinidad. Even conservative journals opposed the governors' attitude and censoriousness, locked as it was in another historical era. The *Sunday Times*, for example, quoted the chair of the Inner London Education Authority's Schools' Committee, Canon Harvey Hinds, as saying: 'The poems are a very sensitive and perceptive assessment of the area where the children are growing up. This old paternalistic and authoritarian Dr Arnold approach is out of date'.[20] Yet there was much more than anachronism at stake, as other observers recognized. In the editorial of the *Teachers' World*,[21] an establishment and professional weekly, the poems themselves became the issue:

> The governors have said that their quality was not the point, the point being merely the fact that Mr. Searle had disobeyed the governors' edict. But why was the edict made? There is at least a suspicion that it was because the poems showed a working-class bias: that is to say, that they drew attention to the conditions under which the working class has to live, and that some of them had inevitable political overtones. Governors wouldn't put it this way: they would say (as indeed they did) that it was a question of 'balance'.

In this sense the pupils had seen the governors' reluctance to have the poems published as a political and cultural attack on their achievement, as well as their right to express their opinions about the place where they lived. Coming from an inner-city area where industrial struggle was common and trade union action a traditional expression of communal assertion and determination – and knowing that dustmen, postmen and dockers had all taken recent action (the spokesman of the parents who joined the rally outside the school gates was a postman) – the students' cultural action had reflected the means that their community and class had used for decades in their struggles for betterment and justice.

But there was more even than this, for the action taken by the students had its own cause in their motivation and ability to write, to be fully and critically literate in order to more fully and consciously understand and begin to change the world around them – in school, street and community. A number of the prime movers of the strike – and some of the poets represented in *Stepney Words* (which soon went into a second issue as well as a reprint, with Ron's cover photograph of a wall poem by Maxine, which read: 'This fire was put out by water. Our fire is in our hearts.') – combined to see their writing at school as a means of making a greater impact on school life than the simple treadmill of examination courses. They began a students' journal which went into a number of issues, dealing with questions like the plight of the local elderly, racism and the struggle against apartheid in South Africa as well as school-based issues like the lack of coherent sex education, and the absurdity of the school uniform and the petty rules enforcing it, 'flesh coloured tights' and all. Profits from the venture went to the Ethiopian Drought Fund, the London Trade Union and Old Age Pensioners' Joint Committee, the Wapping Parents' Action Group and a local drugs rehabilitation centre (*Stepney Words* had included a number of very critical poems about the growing menace of addictive drugs). Writing in the teachers' journal *Radical Education* in 1974, editor of the Sir John Cass students' journal and future professional journalist Tony Harcup described it as

> a unique and important venture. The confidence given to kids by seeing their work in print is obvious, and the interest the magazine created was great. We were supposed to let the Headmaster read it before we printed, but we sold him a copy when we sold copies to everybody else.
>
> We believe our magazine challenged the dictatorial position of the Headmaster and governors of our school; not through including swear words and pictures of tits 'n' bums like university rag mags; but by producing a magazine for kids, expressing the ideas and talents of the kids. And kids' ideas do not always please our governors, as the *Stepney Words* affair showed.[22]

In the wake of the controversy, Adrian Mitchell invited a group of the young poets to a performance of his play about the life of Blake, *Tyger*, by the National Theatre Company. During its denouement, the actors called them onto the stage. It was one of many moments provoked by *Stepney Words*, and the poems were recited by their writers in many London venues, from anti-racist events to local council estate fêtes. They were invited to read as part of 'Poetry International 72' at the Institute of Contemporary Arts and the Young Vic, alongside such luminous writers as Seamus Heaney, John Betjeman, Edward Brathwaite, Robert Lowell, Germaine Greer, Gregory Corso, Adrian Henri and the German 'breath' poet Gerard Ruhm, whom they befriended and who insisted on coming back with them to East London. Ironically, the most prestigious voice of the event was that of the, by that time, very aged W.H. Auden – who, we remember, wrote that 'poetry makes nothing happen'. *Stepney Words* had told another story.

Looking back now at the long and exhaustive hearings that took place as part of the legal and quasi-legal proceedings that finally resulted in my reinstatement in the school after the local education authority (the Inner London Education Authority) had decided to support my case against the governors, they read as an extraordinary documentation not only of 'the spirit of the age', but of the force of poetry, of the extraordinary impact of a few poems written by a group of East London schoolchildren in a creative writing class in one obscure school. In his submission to the first hearing, Trevor Huddleston wrote of the affair as an illustration of a huge movement in attitudes towards vested authority: 'We live at a time when the whole concept of authority in society, in church and in institutions is in revolutionary change. It is quite unrealistic to expect either young teachers or their pupils to be unaffected by this situation', he attested, citing the poetry, the strike, and my own refusal to accept the governors' censoriousness as evidence. But it was also my old English teacher Norman Hidden's remarks at the same hearing, on the effect and value of creative literacy and the writing of poetry in the classroom in particular, that showed how a poem itself could be the basis of a personal source of transformation for a young writer, with the collective action taken by the community of *Stepney Words* poets and their schoolmates as the direct consequence:

> There are a very large number of pupils whose work is represented here, and that seems very significant. It is not just a showpiece of a few of the 'better' children, as it were, this was a really balanced picture of a wide range of children.
> Mostly the poems came from a person feeling that there is some kind of problem that they want to look at to get out of themselves, to objectify it and make it more handleable by objectifying it in this way.
> It is as much a problem of his [*sic*] own creative urge as anything in life can be. And for that child to have his work published might be the thing that really saves him, makes a new person of him, quite apart from the effect that it would have on his academic work and his grasp of English.[23]

And when one of the governors suggested to him that poetry in the classroom should not be 'deliberate social comment' but more an activity of fun, Hidden replied:

> Poetry is both. It is a kind of game that one plays with words, but one plays within the rules of the game. One of the rules of the game is honesty and truth. The best and greatest poetry always has been that which is produced honestly, with truth and sincerity. I can only say that this presentation, *Stepney Words*, contains the qualities of freshness and honesty and sincerity on the part of the children writing which is the most valuable thing about it.

To hear such comments about children's poetry, its purpose, motivation and effect, at a formal and solemn quasi-legal hearing in a City of London oak-panelled executive boardroom, in the midst of grey-suited men who controlled the educational opportunities of hundreds of East London working-class children seemed almost an absurdity in itself, yet everybody there knew, from opposing and entirely different perspectives, that it was the brave and rebellious action of the young poets themselves and their friends that had led directly to our being there. These young people had audaciously rocked the educational and cultural establishment with their words, striking a blow for poetry and critical and creative literacy in a context where its development had seemed as problematic as it could ever be. Their actions and commitment made a nonsense of what was to be declared four years hence in the government's Bullock Report on English in schools, *A Language for Life*: that poetry was 'certainly, outside the current of normal life' and was 'either numinous' or 'an object of derision'.[24] It took the insights of seasoned writers who were kindred spirits of these children, like Colin McInnes, to understand how their 'often startling' words had created a book 'in which poetry is restored to its primal function of revealing a social-political situation to us'.[25] The children's deeds had followed their words, and were to become harbingers of similar school student action that would spread across schools in Britain over the next two decades.

Notes

1 Chris Searle, *The Forsaken Lover: White Words and Black People*, Routledge & Kegan Paul, London, 1972.
2 Majorie L. Hourd and Gertrude E. Cooper, *Coming into their Own*, Heinemann, London, 1971.
3 This, and following quotations are from *Stepney Words*, Reality Press, London, 1971.
4 From a letter from Professor James Britton to Chris Searle, 12 May 1971.
5 Review by Richard Burns, *Times Educational Supplement*, 16 July 1972.
6 Paulo Freire, *Education: The Practice of Freedom*, Writers and Readers Cooperative, London, 1974.
7 Report in the *Times Educational Supplement*, 28 May 1976.
8 From correspondence in legal documentation and transcript of proceedings of the Special Meeting of the Governing Body of Sir John Cass' Foundation and Red Coat Church of England Secondary School, 28 February–3 March 1972.
9 Jack Dash, *Good Morning Brothers!*, Lawrence & Wishart, London, 1969.
10 Trevor Huddleston, *Naught for Your Comfort*, Collins, London, 1956.
11 Trevor Huddleston, *Education and Human Rights*, National Union of Teachers, London, 1969.
12 Letter from Sir Alec Clegg, *Times Educational Supplement*, 18 June 1971.
13 D.J. Enright, 'Children's Hour', *Encounter*, November 1971.
14 Adrian Mitchell, 'Poetry Lives', *Sunday Times*, 13 February 1972.
15 David Holbrook, 'Pearls in Stepney', *Books and Bookmen*, June 1972.
16 Tony Harcup, 'Class Action for Poetic Justice', *New Statesmen and Society*, 31 May 1996.
17 From correspondence in legal documentation and transcript proceedings, op. cit.
18 From *Tribune*, 18 June 1971.

19 Chris Searle: 'Proper Words and Common Words' in *All Our Words*, Young World Books, London, 1986.
20 *Sunday Times*, 30 May 1971.
21 'Comment', *Teachers World*, 1 June 1971.
22 From article in *Radical Education*, winter 1974–5.
23 This and following quotations from correspondence in legal documentation and transcript proceedings, op. cit.
24 *A Language for Life*, The Report of the Bullock Committee, HMSO, London, 1975.
25 Colin McInnes, 'Fighting Words' in the *Times Educational Supplement*, 21 September 1973.

3

FERNDALE FIRES

Mel Robinson's cover to Ferndale Fires

On a Monday afternoon in November 1973 a large group of protesting black and white tenants from two South London housing blocks arrived at Lambeth Housing Department. They were there to express their disgust at the living conditions of the flats in Edward Henry House and Ferndale Court in Brixton. Within the delegation were a large number of women and children, who stayed demonstrating and occupying the offices for the entire afternoon, seeking an interview with the head of the housing department. The *Black Voice*[1] reported that the tenants of both blocks exchanged experiences, telling of the details of life and conditions in their flats, while housing officers called the police. Both Ferndale Court and Edward Henry House were designated 'halfway houses', where tenants were given temporary lets for a few months, before (in theory) being offered better and permanent council accommodation.

A particular dissatisfaction of the Ferndale tenants, many of whom, despite the promises of a better place to live, had been living in the block for up to seven years, was the lack of any form of central heating. Since the conversion to North Sea gas, when the old gas fire appliances had been removed and not replaced, the flats had remained without any form of heating and had become increasingly damp and more and more unhealthy. Families with up to seven children were living in cold and cramped units, often with bathroom and kitchen facilities combined in the same small room, and their Lambeth Council landlords were doing little to provide either relief or improvement. Each flat had just a single electricity socket in the living room, so electric heaters could be used in this room only, causing whole families to move their bedding and sleep there, while the other rooms deteriorated, becoming more and more damp and unhealthy.

The protesting tenants returned to attend a council meeting on local housing later that evening at Lambeth Town Hall. Their protests managed to force a promise from the council of an allocation of £21,000, to ensure that all the children's bedroooms in Ferndale Court had an electricity point installed, but nothing more. No progress was made regarding their main demand, which was a swift rehousing to better and more healthy council accommodation away from Ferndale Court and Edward Henry House.

As a teacher at a local primary school close to Ferndale Court, I had heard of conditions there from another source – my own students, who frequently came to school tired and cold, complaining of another virtually sleepless night or an uncomfortable evening. As the nights closed in and the weather became colder in the autumn, their morning stories during registration began to have an increasingly similar and angry theme. A number of 10-year-olds were unhappy that their parents had no other choice but to use paraffin stoves, which emitted lingering fumes around their flats and which were temperamental and dangerous. Sometimes the wicks would burn down prematurely, sending out choking clouds of toxic black smoke into the room, and their precarious stands made it easy for them to be knocked over, particularly if there were children playing around them.

Inevitably, a serious accident happened, then another. The baby brother of one of the final year Jamaican students was badly burned, and then one of the students themselves was burned in a paraffin stove fire that completely burned out his family's flat. I remember visiting the home and being deeply shocked by the extent of the damage, with the black and grey dirt from the smoke completely covering the walls. As teachers we felt we should be helping the parents directly, not only by standing up as trade unionists for their campaign, but also in a curriculum sense, by trying to deal with these issues of danger, oppression and protest that were so central to our students' lives, both in and out of school. The fires were the most painful and immediate manifestation of injustice in their lives, but they related to the other menaces that surrounded their own and their families' experiences in and around Brixton. Their relationship with the local police and its policy of stopping and harassing young black people, particularly our students' older brothers, was very much in the forefront of their minds.

I asked my students to try to write down in poetry what they felt about what was happening in their lives. Ten-year-old Rachel wrote this:

> Brixton is a dirty place
> Just like South London,
> Where the police are always on the chase.
> Some people get killed
> Some get hurt,
> But still the people go on and on –
> When the police see you on the run
> They say you are a suspect.[2]

A group of girls collaborated on a chant-poem which they recited together across the classroom:

> Brixton has pollution speading all around
> You want to see the people winding round the town,
> Buying egg and bacon, buying coffee and tea,
> Buying ackee and saltfish just for you and me.
> Dutch pot pan frying, pan pan stove
> Whenever you see us running we must be doing the
>   Jamaica jive!
>
> *Chorus*: Jamaica! (*seven times*)
>
> You want to see the policeman with his bandaman stick,
> He love to threaten people, but we can put him in a fix!
>
> *Chorus*
>
> You want to hear the traffic when it gets stuck,
> It is like a bulldozer on top of a truck.
>
> *Chorus*

You want to hear the fire engine rolling down the street
It is just like a banjo man playing his tamboreen!

Chorus

Evoking Jamaica was common and popular. Although the class was multiracial, there was a very strong group of Jamaican girls who often set its daily ethos. Many of these girls had either grown up in or visited Jamaica, and often expressed a strong and living sense of nostalgia for how they remembered it, tending to idealize the island in a continuing comparison to inner city and often inhospitable Brixton. Maria wrote her own poem of comparison:

Once upon a time ago
I used to be in the sunshine of Jamaica,
But now I'm under the dirty flats of Brixton.
Brixton! Yha!
I wish I was over the sea with my lovely Jamaica,
Fights go on
Police after boys
And I wish I was in Jamaica.
But maybe some day
I'll come back to Jamaica.
And see the lovely beach
And smell my sweet scent of Jamaica.

There was escapism here, a flight from the streets, the iron bars and gates of Ferndale Court, the stoves and the fires. It started a sense of emulation among the students, with others thinking of their own country and family origin, and of how to express its virtues or beauties. This brought us on to the idea of a contest, a mock 'beauty contest', where the theme of the features of 'their countries' in short four-line stanzas would replace the notion of a market of young women. A girl from Barbados wrote:

I am Miss Barbados
I love the sugar cane
I hear the wind blow off the beach
And the deep blue sea sing.

A Jamaican girl who had been living in New York with her grandparents, and who had now moved to be with her mother in Ferndale Court, wrote:

I am Miss U.S.A.
Far across the sea,
Where the tall buildings
Fly as high as me!

A Nigerian girl responded, with pride and confidence:

> I am Miss Africa
> A continent wide and huge,
> Of hot dry deserts and wide open plains
> And rivers filled with forest rains.

And none of this prepared the students for the lines of a quiet white girl whom everybody in her class assumed was born and had lived her life in the local streets around Brixton. But in her few lines she had another story, another place, to tell:

> I am Miss Belfast
> I come from a noisy place,
> I hear the bullets in my ears
> And I shake as the bombs hit my face.

The contest threw up dialogue and surprises, as well as challenges and a new curriculum of the collective memory and real places. Yet the class kept returning to the fires; their dangers and menace. It was as if paraffin had become a venom in their lives. I decided to attempt to write a play which incorporated some of the students' verses about Brixton, which used the motif of the transformed 'beauty contest', but which had as its main theme the paraffin stove fires and the tenants' resistance to the conditions which caused them. For not only were there protests developing among the parents whose children came to the school, in the form of the occupation of the housing offices, but a tenants' action group had been formed and a rent strike for proper heating facilities had begun. These actions by the parents could only be strengthened and helped by the support of their children's school, to ensure that the curriculum responded to the exigencies of the lives of its students, giving an affirmation to the brave and necessary actions of their parents.

The play dramatized the children's response to the fires and their parents' protest, but sought also to underline the internationalism of the school. It also allowed the students to speak in their own particular dialects and took its incidents from events narrated in the classroom. The last act, for example, involved a fight between two boys, using sticks and dustbin lids as shields – a scene graphically described by a girl one morning. The fight is interrupted by yet another fire and a call to all the tenants to unite and assemble for an immediate protest march to the town hall. The play ended with the residents, young and old, marching off.

The play was performed in the classroom and to the rest of the school, and later at a protest meeting at a local church hall called by the tenants action group and the local black workers' movement. But the cultural action went further. A teaching colleague, Mel Robinson, and myself changed the play script into a children's story for publication. Mel was the music teacher at the school, as well as being a brilliant artist. He had already provided a melody for one of the students' poems and thus given the short play a musical dimension. Now he added some superbly evocative black and white illustrations for the book, which we named after the play: *Ferndale Fires*. These images caught the anguish and pain of the experiences described in the book, as well as the children's intelligence, humour and creative energy. The book was launched in the teachers' centre next to the school, with an evening of music and poetry from the students themselves, as well as invited speakers and poets like John La Rose, Andrew Salkey and Linton Kwesi Johnson.[3] The great Barbadian poet Edward Kamau Brathwaite sent a congratulatory letter, commending in particular the 'touching testaments' of the children.[4] The event also gave a platform for the Ferndale tenants, and any profits made by the publication were directed to their action group and a local community bookshop that had recently been established in Brixton.

Ferndale Fires was intended to be a curriculum project of cultural action, and it proved so to be – drawing together the work of the classroom with a particular struggle involving the students and their families outside the school: the reconciliation of curriculum and community. It contrasted starkly with the books used in the school to teach the students how to read. These were the 'Peter and Jane' Ladybird series. In these books the two middle class, white, young protagonists move in a world of neat suburban housing, private cars, red setter dogs, holidays by the seaside, rich relatives like Mr White who live in huge country houses, and friendly neighbourhood policemen. 'I like the police', says Peter. 'They help you'. Nothing could have been more distant and alien to the lives of the children of Ferndale Court. *Ferndale Fires* sought to reflect that world of the doorstep, and in doing so, exchange dislocation of experience for authenticity, phantom children for real children.

Within and around the school there was much support for and pleasure taken in the book. But further afield it was greeted with hostility. Whereas the local black community bulletin, *Freedom News*[5] recognized it as 'a community tale coming true because the pressures it bases itself on are true', and *Time Out*[6] insightfully described the book as 'an example of imagination turned on to reality to transform it in such a way as to look back at reality with enlightened eyes', the children's books editor of *The Times*[7] was much more circumspect. It seemed to him that for a teacher to give unambiguous support to a group of his students' parents and develop that support in a classroom context, was to be 'tractarian' (i.e. propagandist). He wrote, in a surprisingly long review of a book which was primarily a 'community' publication:

> *Ferndale Fires* is a raw book, which does not care much for the niceties of literary construction, and which in its narrow tendentiousness resembles nothing so much as the tracts with which the Victorians fed the working classes. It does not seek to argue the realities it presents, and one may question whether the child reader is being told the whole truth. Can local councils be blamed for parental irresponsibility? By what order of priorities are tenants deprived of their central heating? The facts, as always, are more complex than the tractarians let on.

Yet even this reviewer added that the book had 'two virtues from which more accomplished writers might learn: the accuracy of much of its dialogue and its sense of the integrity of childhood'. A 'crude authenticity' about the book was also conceded.

The anxieties that many teachers felt about a critical literacy approach which provoked cultural action, were openly expressed as a direct result of the publication of *Ferndale Fires*. I wrote a short article for *The Teacher*,[8] the weekly journal of my union, the National Union of Teachers, explaining rather as I have here, the way in which the book developed, as a direct consequence of the students' worries about the fires and their parents' direct action to better their housing conditions. A teacher from Bradford Grammar School wrote into the following week's issue of the journal, suggesting that I had been 'prodding' the Ferndale parents into action (rather than reflecting and affirming their resistance): 'I also wonder if they will be compelled to pay extra for the "proper central heating" they now demand' he declared.[9]

Critical literacy means not only helping the student become conscious of the inequalities surrounding or pressing down upon her or his world, but supporting the means his or her community takes to challenge and overcome them. That is central to the 'cultural action' that the student takes. This is what I tried to explain in my reply to the Bradford teacher's letter, pointing out also that the teacher's 'own working conditions are obviously improved if his pupils come to school after enjoying the basic comforts of properly equipped and heated housing'. I went on to make the point that:

> the teacher should support and affirm any such struggle of his pupils or their parents, by introducing elements of that struggle into the classroom, and relating the activities in his classroom to the campaign – adding his supportive skills of organisation and articulacy, and encouraging the participation of his pupils.[10]

Yet such principles broke with the notion of 'neutrality' and 'objectivity' that were still at the centre of the traditional view of the role of the teacher in English schools, and to which most teachers of 'English' had always attached themselves. Critical literacy, with its organic link to cultural action was very 'un-English' in this regard. It was not that most English teachers did not want change, or did not want betterment for their working-class students. It was that the pursuit of that change could only legitimately come *after* not *while* the process of literacy teaching was under way. In the same way, education was not the process of change in itself, but the prelude to change. You become literate, you get your education, *before* you set about the process of change. The idea that the classroom act of literacy was a part of the process of transformation in itself and legitimately so, was something that many teachers resisted, blocked in the mindset that education was about knowledge detached from action, rather than knowledge as the inseparable guide and dynamo of action.

The contestation among teachers around this point was illustrated again in a further contribution to the letters page of *The Teacher*, when another correspondent took up my arguments in the letter of the week before:

Sir: Why isn't Mr. Searle more honest? Why doesn't he admit that he's using his school, the children and his own position as a teacher as an outlet for his own politics?

The parents of many children in my school work at a well-known motor car factory. When they are on strike should I 'support and affirm' their action as Mr. Searle does by getting them to write politically slanted poems? This is to politicise education with a vengeance.

And what nonsense it is to say that 'education is primarily involved in eroding, fighting against and triumphing over the immediate and historical inequalities facing the majority of our children'. Education is *primarily* involved with teaching the skills of literacy and Mr. Searle would serve his working class and immigrant parents better if he attended to that rather than his own politics.[11]

The nub is in these words. For any teacher adopting an approach of critical literacy is going to meet these accusations and arguments continually – that you are proselytizing, indoctrinating, politicizing etc., that you are simply imposing you own views on young minds, that you are a Pied Piper, a brainwasher. I have certainly been called all these and much more by those who see education and literacy simply marking time with the status quo, and not integral to the process of action and change. My answer to this letter from the teacher who taught the children of Ford workers was to argue the case I would always argue – that the teachers *learn* from the experience of working people struggling for change and betterment, and the lessons they learn can be applied to their own pedagogy and be at the heart of their curriculum:

Perhaps he [sic] should consider the record of resistance to consistent exploitation and injustice that the parents of his own students, and their workmates past and present, have achieved. He may learn far more about our own possibilities as teachers as an organised workforce, as well as some very potent material available for his own classes.[12]

So for me, *Ferndale Fires* provoked as much thought and debate about the teacher's role in supporting his or her students and the vital connection between classroom and community – and the curriculum that unites them – as it did about the struggle for better housing and safety for children in the home. What it taught me was that all these things are faces of the same reality, the reality that must be at the centre of what we mean by educational progress and all our lives at school.

Notes

1 *Black Voice*, 5 (1), 1974.
2 These, and other quoted poems are from Chris Searle and Mel Robinson, *Ferndale Fires*, Reality Press, London, 1974.

3 See reports of the launch in the *Times Educational Supplement*, 29 March 1974, and the *West Indian World*, 19 April 1974.
4 Letter from Edward Kamau Brathwaite to Chris Searle, 15 March 1974.
5 *Freedom News*, 15 December 1973.
6 *Time Out*, 29 March 1974.
7 *The Times*, 13 March 1974.
8 *The Teacher*, 8 March 1974.
9 *The Teacher*, 22 March 1974.
10 *The Teacher*, 9 April 1974.
11 *The Teacher*, 26 April 1974.
12 *The Teacher*, 10 May 1974.

THE BASEMENT:
POETRY'S OPEN DOOR

Ron McCormick's cover to The Boxer Speaks

The furore of cultural protest and action that surrounded the suppression of *Stepney Words* and also the strong public support and protest on its behalf, helped to create a new interest and appetite for poetry and creative writing in the East London neighbourhoods where its young authors lived. Suddenly it seemed credible for teenagers to be poets; poetry had shed both its mystique and its mystification. It had overcome Adrian Mitchell's dictum that 'most people don't like poetry because poetry doesn't like most people'. Now these young Blakes were proudly exposing their work. When hundreds of them had protested and marched through their own East End streets, then onwards through the business and financial centre of the City of London, past St Paul's Cathedral to the West End in pursuit of the prime minister, they were marching for poetry and proudly carried a poem at the head of their procession. They were following the route of many such protest marches before them, from the 1887 demonstration of the unemployed which was attacked by police on horses and when one of the thousands of marchers, Alfred Linnell – a jobless worker from Bow – was killed, to the dockers of 1889 and the East London suffragettes. All these protest movements had inspired poetry, with William Morris reading at Linnell's funeral, the poet-dockers publishing their work in local journals and broadsheets, and the suffragettes' passionate creativity finding voice within the pages of Sylvia Pankhurst's *Women's Dreadnaught*.

The school students' 1971 protest had won me back my job at Sir John Cass and Red Coat School. It took me nearly two years of legal contest which had taken me from the law courts in the Strand to tribunals in City boardrooms, but supported by the National Union of Teachers, the Inner London Education Authority, the National Council for Civil Liberties and many generous individuals, I was able to walk back into the school in May 1973 and continue my teaching.

The two years out of the school meant that many of my ex-students and the poets of *Stepney Words* had left the school, and the timetable I now had to follow gave me little opportunity to consolidate in the classroom the work of two years before with the same young writers. I still met them informally out of school, and a strong group continued with their writing, but we had nothing institutional to support it beyond the journal that some of them had begun at school during their sixth form.

Stepney Words had gone into several re-printings and had finally been adopted by the pioneering community 'Centerprise' bookshop in Hackney, so we had raised enough money to undertake further publishing. Since a number of poems by old age pensioners had been sent to us, Ron McCormick and I combined to produce a book of their poems called *Elders*,[1] in order to raise funds for the London Trade Union and Old Age Pensioners Committee, who were campaigning for an increase in the state pension. One of the elderly poets who sent us some of his work was an ex-boxer, Stephen 'Johnny' Hicks. Stephen, who had been born in Stepney in 1906, and who had boxed professionally through the 1930s before becoming a factory worker and building labourer, had turned to poetry in his late years, 'juggling about with rhymes and limericks to break the monotony of the work'. He once wrote that:

It seems that somewhere within me
a silent voice now and then says,
'Hurry please, let everything be,
and pick up your paper and pen.'[2]

His poetry was sharp, witty and frequently very stark and moving, recalling his boxing days and interspersing surrealistic fantasy with biting commentary on the conditions facing old age pensioners. In *Elders*, we published his 'Economic Pensioner':

Economic Pensioner

I have just turned sixty five
An uneventful day,
But thankful to be still alive
To draw my first week's pay.

I have to really understand
Which food I wish to buy,
Because I cannot live too grand
With prices up so high.

So what I'll do with every hour
As I'll be so hard pressed,
Is rack my brains to find out how
To spend my money best.

I cannot live in clover
For I hardly have enough,
And there won't be much left over
When I've bought all my stuff.

So when my week's pay out has gone
And my resistance too,
Alas, I'll have to struggle on
Just like the others do.

This poem, and another, the anonymous 'Kate's Poem' – found by a nurse in the hospital bedside locker of a mute octogenarian woman after she died – had a profound effect on the students at school, and in particular the young writers of *Stepney Words* who were still there. 'Kate's Poem' had a universality and directness which penetrated deeply into young minds:

Kate's Poem

What do you see nurses
What do you see?

Are you thinking
    when you're looking at me,
A crabbit old woman
    not very wise,
Uncertain of habit
    with far-away eyes,
Who dribbles her food
    and makes no reply,
When you say in a loud voice
    'I do wish you'd try',
Who seems not to notice
    the things that you do,
And forever is losing
    a stocking or shoe,
Who unresisting or not
    lets you do as you will
With bathing and feeding
    the long day to fill.
Is that what you're thinking,
    is that what you see?
Then open your eyes nurse,
    you're not looking at me.
I'll tell you who I am
    as I sit here so still,
As I use at your bidding
    as I eat at your will.
I'm a small child of ten
    with a father and mother,
Brothers and sisters
    who love one another,
A young girl at sixteen
    with wings on her feet,
Dreaming that soon now
    a lover she'll meet.
A bride soon at twenty,
    my heart gives a leap
Remembering the vows
    that I promise to keep.
At twenty-five now
    I have young of my own
Who need me to build
    a secure, happy home.
A young woman of thirty
    my young now grow fast,
Bound to each other
    with ties that should last.
At forty my young ones

now grown will soon be gone,
But my man stays beside me
    to see I don't mourn.
At fifty once more
    babies play round my knee,
Again we know children
    my loved one and me.
Dark days are upon me,
    my husband is dead,
I look at the future
    I shudder with dread,
For my young are all busy
    rearing young of their own,
And I think of the years
    and the love I have known.
I'm an old woman now
    and nature is cruel,
'Tis her jest to make
    old age look like a fool.
The body it crumbles
    grace and vigour depart,
There now is a stone
    where once I had a heart:
But inside this old carcase
    a young girl still dwells,
And now and again
    my battered heart swells.
I remember the joys,
    I remember the pain,
And I'm loving and living
    life over again.
I think of the years
    all too few – gone too fast,
And accept the stark fact
    that nothing can last.
So open your eyes, nurses,
    open and see,
Not a crabbit old woman,
    look closer – see ME![3]

In his autobiography *Sparring for Luck*,[4] which was published posthumously
in 1982, Stephen Hicks wrote about the circumstances that caused him to
submit his poems for the *Elders* anthology:

July of 1971 came and went and at the retiring age of sixty five I became
a state pensioner with nothing to do but write. I had been reading about
the publication of a book of children's poems called *Stepney Words*,

compiled by local schoolteacher Christopher Searle. It was published without the permission of governors, and for this 'wicked' deed Chris was sacked. During my lifetime I have heard of some fantastic and weird decisions, but this one excelled them all. Just imagine getting the sack for teaching good English poetry. I reckon if William Shakespeare had been around at this time he would have joined the schoolchildren's strike which ultimately followed. Seven hundred children came out on strike opposing the dismissal and the news media highlighted the event too. However, all's well that end's well, but it took a strike to decide whether or not poetry was for the good interest of children. It was quite logical to me that with poetry in the news for a change, I should send a few of my own to Chris Searle just for fun . . .

What was significant was that poetry had spread from classroom to community, and there was now a way and mechanism to publish it. Stephen's poems in *Elders* fascinated the young writers still at Sir John Cass' School. A group of them went to visit him regularly in their lunch hour: they befriended him, painted his grim flat in a tenement building on Stepney Green, listened to his boxing stories and memories of the 1930s and did their best to persuade him to get proper medical attention for his seriously ulcerated leg. 'It is a joy to speak to them', he wrote in *Sparring for Luck*, and in a strange and human way, he became a hero to them, a symbol of past struggle and present stamina. When the 'Basement Writers' group began in October 1973, and we were discussing whose poetry should form the first published book, none of the young writers wanted to push themselves or each others' work. 'Let's do Stephen's poetry', they declared unanimously, 'his is the most important'. And the effect of his poetry became exemplary: his use of rhymes, couplets, puns, and four-line stanzas, were all emulated by the younger poets in their own work.

I remember these moments with clarity because they signalled an empathy from the young to the old which was one of the most telling features of the Basement Writers, and which had also been a theme of many of the poems in *Stepney Words*. Tony Harcup, a Sir John Cass student, one of the Basement pioneers and the son of a beefeater in the Tower of London, wrote this moving tribute to his friend Stephen, which was included in his collection *Never had it so Good,*[5] the next book published after Stephen's book of poems. It could almost have been Stephen writing a poem about his own life:

The Fighter (for Stephen Hicks)

Searching for satisfaction all his life,
Unemployment, poverty, and strife.
Living alone, now, in one small room,
The old age pension don't lift the gloom.

His friends pop in to speak a while,
And when he sees them coming he's happy
        and he smiles.

He talks about past times, both good
        and bad,
And seeing him so lively makes his friends
        so glad.

He shows his friends certificates and old
        school reports,
Photos and press cuttings of the boxers
        he has fought.
He thanks his friends for sparing the time
        and he talks about his poems,
He smiles and laughs, but must be a bit sad
        when his friends are going.

But we love going to see him, and we're always
        glad we do,
He's a great bloke and poet, I know you'd
        love him too.
It's really great for us to see his big
        blue eyes alight.
Even though he's finished boxing
        he'll never end his fight.

Searching for satisfaction all his life,
Unemployment, poverty, and strife.
Living alone, now in one small room,
The old age pension don't lift the gloom.

As for Stephen himself, he was overwhelmed that his own work was to find published form – paid for, of course, from the proceeds of *Stepney Words*:

Just imagine, a book solely devoted to one thing – my poetry. It was hardly believable, the first one of a whole collection of anthologies by authors of the Basement Writers, so-called because they met in the basement of St. George's Town Hall in Cable Street. The group consisted at first mainly of Chris' pupils and ex-pupils who wanted to continue their writing activities outside of school. The group soon grew though to include writers of all ages from the surrounding area.[6]

Stephen's account is an accurate one and shows how selflessly these young writers saw their priorities. The mobilization of words was being provoked by the mobilization of friendship, admiration and love for an old neighbour. It was *his* achievement they wanted to see in print – just as, years later, some of them combined to edit and publish his autobiography. As for Stephen, his enthusiasm for poetry was taking off with even greater force, particularly within the ex-boxers community, where he was recognized as their bard. He contributed a poem to every edition of their news-sheet *Seconds Out*, and, as we have seen, wrote in *Sparring for Luck* of his excitement at the publication of his poems. He made them reach his own heroes too:

> So it came about during early March 1994 that my book of poems was published and I was the author. It was entitled *The Boxer Speaks* and many of them were sold by the Basement Writers. The London Ex-Boxers Association of which I was a member bought four hunded and presented one to Jack Dempsey, former World Heavyweight boxing champion, 1919–1926. I got a letter from him in response to reading my poetry, with a coloured picture with the words 'Good luck Steve. Keep the good work up. Jack Dempsey.'

The Boxer Speaks set off a process of creative writing and community publishing that had been born in the classroom poems of *Stepney Words* and moved out into the heart of the East London community. In the concrete, low-ceilinged basement of St George's Town Hall, accessible only by a narrow staircase outside the only window, where the writers could see the tentative legs and lower trunk of anyone descending, but no more, the writers read and discussed their work, and planned future publications and public readings. The venue itself was historic. It overlooked the shell of St George's Church, shattered by Nazi bombs in the Second World War, and outside in Cable Street, thousands of anti-fascists had stopped the march of Sir Oswald Mosley's blackshirts in October 1936. The writers arrived, sometimes boldly, sometimes shyly and self-consciously, wondering what they would find, for it was something they had never known before. We sat in a circle, taking turns to read our work, and volunteering comment and criticism. The first members were some of the *Stepney Words* poets, plus Leslie Mildiner and Bill House, two co-authors of an extraordinary novel called *The Gates*[7] shortly to be published locally by Centerprise. They were school-phobics, so if the Basement had represented anything like a traditional school ethos, they would have soon abandoned it. Gradually other, older writers came: Gladys McGee, the mother of Kim, whose poem 'The Old Bird' had been in *Stepney Words*, and Jim Wolveridge, who ran a paperback bookstall in Whitechapel Market. He was an authority on cockney language and slang, and his books *Aint it Grand*[8] and *The Muvver Tongue*[9] were soon to find print.

The Basement's first publication – which we completed while we were typesetting Stephen's book – was a poetry poster which we posted on walls, billboards, and hoardings all over Stepney. It included poems which set the political and thematic context for the group. One described the speculation and money-making in the new East End, the building of expensive new hotels, wharves for luxury yachts and new gentrified housing while 'the pensioners, the homeless, the school services, all are perishing'. Another, by Keith, a black young writer from Wapping, condemned the new anti trade union laws, while Costas, a Greek Cypriot included his poem 'Birthplace', condemning the stranglehold of the fascist junta in Greece. Other lyrical poems reflected upon childhood, upon friendship and love. Another writer created new lyrics to 'Maybe It's because I'm a Londoner', seen from the perspective of a pensioner 'on the 23rd sad and lonely floor' of a council tower block. In the centre was a poem by Stephen Hicks, praising the strength and resilience of local working-class people. Another, by a young playwright, Billy Colvill, who was to write some outstanding plays for the Half Moon Theatre in Stepney over the next few years, described the world that the writers saw all around them, and the questions they were asking – storing up and reflecting upon their insights through poetry in the hope of eventual answers:

> I see
> a woman at the social security
> with two kids,
> screaming for money
> That means something.
>
> I see
> in the paper,
> that the miners
> won't give in;
> That means something.
>
> I see
> lovers laying on the grass
> like barbed wire;
> That means something.
>
> I see a drunk
> looking down the road;
> That means something;
> and when I know what it means
> then I'll mean something
> and when I mean something
> then; I'll hit back.[10]

And it meant something for people to stop and curiously read such words as they passed, next to glaring advertisements, local election posters, or notices for demolition. The 'second poetry poster'[11] soon followed, with tender love poems and adolescent urgings fused with rhymes of indignation on the fate of the nearby London docks:

> When I look from my door on the fourth floor,
> I can see in the distance the Tower Hotel
> Where rich dwell on land we did not sell!!

Statements by middle-aged Second World War veterans about the dangers of a new fascism:

Have you read *Mein Kampf*?
You should. It tells you why
So many of the world's young men
were marched, and forced to die.
They started with a slogan,
'Our Nation First' it said
Then 'tainted blood must be cleansed'.
They left six million dead.

Eddie Baunton

found themselves next to epigrams which told stories in the most startling and succinct of verses:

Silence, they tell me
                is golden.
Is that why we don't speak
now I wear your ring?

Debbie Carnegie

And there were poems that stopped school students as they passed, founded upon real observations and reaching the heart of disaffection and dissatisfaction with school:

Second Year Defeat

Rude words on the blackboard
crushed chalk on the floor.
Books out of the window,
run out, bang the door.

Teacher's depression
me and my class
football in the playground
connects with school glass

Cigarettes in the toilet
Nudie books too.
When I leave this dump
then what will I do?

Work on the railways?
A stall down The Lane?
Empty the bins
Or clean out a drain?

I'm nothing special
the school's told me that,
I aint got no brains
and my prospects are flat

Can't hit back at the system,
it's blank, has no features,
So while I'm at school
I'll take it out on the teachers.

Alan Gilbey

This was people's poetry – comprehensible, relevant, sharply pertinent and observant, and full of humour, passion and sometimes anguish. A string of small 32-page poetry editions followed *The Boxer Speaks*, accompanied by the weekly sessions in the Basement and regular open readings at the Half Moon Theatre. Special celebratory and benefit readings were organized too: to remember the life and poetry of Isaac Rosenberg, the Stepney poet killed in the trenches in the last days of the First World War; in solidarity with the imprisoned Shrewsbury building workers; to commemorate the fortieth anniversary of the Battle of Cable Street; to support the campaign against docklands redevelopment profiteering and speculation; in support of Tony Soares, an imprisoned black activist. Some of these events held unforgettable moments: Jack Dash reading his poems in the manner of his strike speeches at the dock gates; the Yiddish lyricism of the veteran Jewish poet, Avram Stencl, reading his poems in memory of his friend Rosenberg; the Barbadian poet Peter Blackman, in his seventies, reading, in full, his epic poem of the 1940s, 'My Song is for All Men'.[12] At the Basement, the meetings were frequently interrupted by surprise and welcome guests: Adrian Mitchell, spending the evening with us and reading from his collection *Ride the Nightmare*; the sudden appearance of a frail, elderly, impeccably-suited man, who politely asked if he could recite from heart the whole of Browning's *The Pied Piper of Hamelin*. He did so, bade his goodbyes, and left. Or the occasional intervention of a wanderer mistaking the Basement for the vagrants' hostel a few buildings further up Cable Street. One such visitor, feeling warmed and welcomed, decided to stay, and obliged with a rendition of a long, rhyming poem in broad Glaswegian about a man searching for justice, but finding none. It was poetry's open door, and any thoughts I could ever have nursed about poetry being detached, elitist, irrelevant to real life or ordinary people, could never have survived such experiences. Poetry became a part of the community bloodstream. It had left its high places, fallen off its shelves into the streets of East London. It had flowed directly from local classrooms, all along the pavements. And it was also returning to those same classrooms, as local teachers ordered copies of the Basement books and used them in their English lessons to stimulate further poetry.

As for the Basement regulars, their confidence and output went from strength to strength, as they benefited from mutual support, empathy and friendly criticism. Gladys McGee had written, after one of her first visits to the Basement, this short poem-plea called 'The Brain':

The Brain

Please read my poetry,
Don't let me write in vain,

Because it's only in the last few years
I found I had a brain.[13]

She was certainly exploiting it to its fullness now, at the age of 60. She wrote poems about the anguish of human relations, satirized bureaucracy and government, remembered childish experiences of hop-picking or, in this vivacious poem, 'Empire Day', ridiculed the imperial pomp and institutional brainwashing of her own schooling:

Empire Day

'I've been picked!
I've been picked'
My arms were a-flinging
And my heart was a-singing
'cos I'd been picked!
It was for Empire Day I'd been picked,
My teacher said I was a good reader
And could dress up as a leader
of the Empire we had then.
And I'd wear a bronze helmet
And be draped in a red, white and blue flag
And reign over all other lands –
That's what an empire meant then.
They day came nearer, I was getting excited
Then my teacher spoke to me
And my day was blighted,
She realized I was too small to reign –
She wanted someone tall and striking
Who looked like a Viking,
Holding a shield and looking across the sea.
I was already weedy
And felt rather seedy
And asked if I could go home,
Because I was in pain.
She said I could do this part when I was older
How could I, silly old cow! –
We aint got no Empire now![14]

Gladys McGee went on to have two books published, make recordings and appear on television and become a favourite of the London poetry cabaret of the 1980s, never losing her satirical bite and vitality.

Sally Flood, an embroidery machinist in a Spitalfields clothing factory, called her anthology *Window on Brick Lane*,[15] as she often wrote her poems while at her machine, sitting overlooking the life of that extraordinary street. She prefaced it with these lines:

> Generations of the exploited
> Are coming alive
> And whispering
> Their dreams.

And poetry was giving volume and shape to their whispers. Sally's poems have a beautiful and most delicately-observed lyricism, which reminded me of some of the poems by the *Stepney Words* children. For example:

City Dweller

> A magpie sat on the garden wall
> Then slowly flapped its wings
> Displayed a breast of black and white
> Rotated round on springs.
> His claws were stuck as if with glue
> So tightly wrenched were they,
> Then suddenly, he raised his back
> Before he flew away.

The poet watches his disappearance, marvelling, empathizing, turning the moment into an always:

> On powerful wings you swooped and dived
> Your destination clear
> No city dweller tied by toil
> No tax had you to fear.
> It took just but a moment
> To catch you in my sight,
> And now I journey with you
> A stowaway in flight.[16]

There was beauty coming from this dark place below the streets, lit by glaring neon lights and furnished with plastic chairs, and unafraid talk of love too. Debbie Carnegie, a young nursery nurse wrote all her poems in bed, so called her anthology *Bedwritten*.[17] Among her short poems of surprise were:

> A balloon bursts and inside there's
> Nothing.
> My heart breaks and inside there's
> Love.

and her reflections touched humour on their way towards bristling insights in the simplest of words:

I wanna go to heaven
But I hate white
Why can't angels sit on rainbows?
I mean, what does Picasso do
among white clouds?

I wanna go to heaven
But I hate harps
Why can't angels play guitars?
I mean, what does Hendrix do
beyond the stars?

The early history of the Basement was a fusion of creative writing and cultural action, right from the outset. Its very beginnings were planted in young people actively helping, befriending and campaigning for the aged. And as their own community was so close to the docklands, their work was projected into the broad protest movement to ensure that whatever developments took place in the huge vacant, derelict acreage surrounding their lives, it would be to their community's benefit. The writers threw themselves into the protest movements against the building of the huge Tower Hotel, the World Trade Centre and the luxury convertions of warehouses to high-price housing for wealthy buyers after Thameside views and up-market new locations. Alan Gilbey, a *Stepney Words* contributor, poet, artist and dramatist composed and drew his first cartoon-comic called *Up the Docks*[18] when he was 15. At 5p it proclaimed itself a 'dirt cheap' buy, and in the manner of the American comic tradition pitched the villainous property speculator 'Taylor Woodrow Slater Walker Proffitgrabber' against the caped hero 'Will of the People'. On the Wapping Pierhead, with Tower Bridge and the Tower Hotel behind them, they confront each other for the ultimate struggle, the 'power of money' against the 'power of the people'. Gilbey's comic sold and was given away to schools and across the local community in its hundreds, and was also adapted into a melodrama and performed at the Half Moon Theatre.

Initially shy and nervous, Gilbey once said that he had walked up and down the pavement outside the Basement a dozen times on its first night, plucking up the courage to come down the steps and take part. Very soon he became one of its most creative elements, writing poems, designing covers and posters illustrating the collections of his co-poets, and organizing performance sessions. One of his most successful posters advertised a demonstration against a 'colour bar' being operated in a local pub, the Railway Hotel in Mile End. You could almost measure the growth in his confidence week by week and so many dimensions of his creativity flourished. His poem 'The Art of Glazing' expressed something thematic about the community function of the Basement Writers, and how they saw their cultural project, so intimately bonded with the people and streets around them. Starting from an English classroom, their utterance had become a voice and conscience of the community, a voice carrying unity and resistance – and mediation too.

The Art of Glazing

There's a workman down that sidestreet,
you might see him as you pass.
He's slowly, but with practised hands,
removing broken glass.
The skill that steers his actions
has been schooled by repetition,
replacing brick broke window panes
(an old East End tradition).
He rarely rates a second glance,
there's just one small child gazing
at the patience and dexterity
of the noble art of glazing.

From the back of an old, battered van
that's often down this street
the man selects a sheet of glass,
then scores and trims it neat.
It fits exactly in the frame,
a knowledgeable knack.
The small child offers him a smile,
the glazier smiles back.
His technique and aesthetics
are not awesome or amazing,
just the everyday and commonplace,
and vital art of glazing.

The child is often Asian,
at times Jewish, sometimes black.
The window man is always there
and always coming back.
The small, important smile they share
is a promise we must keep,
to kick our own complacency
and sacrifice some sleep.
To watch over the wounded
and to douse the fire that's blazing,
and set aside a little time
to learn the art of glazing.[19]

Writers like Alan Gilbey took their various routes, and others took their place in those Tuesday night sessions, and have been doing so ever since. For in 1997 the 'Basement Writers' is now in its twenty-fifth year. Gladys McGee and Sally Flood took the helm when many of the younger writers dispersed. Harcup migrated to Leeds, became a freelance journalist and eventually a major force behind the *Leeds Other Paper*, a pioneer community journal.

Gilbey became a radio and theatre playwright, a performance poet on the London circuit and cartoon animator. Kim McGee and Leslie Mildiner left for Canada, Leslie to Vancouver where he reads his work professionally, and Kim to Toronto, where she entertains children and teaches through puppetry and performance. Other writers, scores of them over a quarter-century, continued the Basement tradition in local and far-flung word-places and word-venues, all taking with them the echoes of Stephen Hicks' brave and fighting words.

Writing 25 years later, Tony Harcup reflected upon the impact of those Tuesday nights at the Basement and the words which were at their centre:

> For me, the most important thing about being involved in the Basement Writers was not the quality of the literature – let's face it, we all produced some embarrassing work among the few pieces of inspired writing – but the fact that it opened up new possibilities. It was a bridge between the classroom and the outside world, a bridge which could and did lead to all sorts of places.
>
> Those attending in the early days when I was involved ranged from people like me doing A Levels to those who had dropped out of school. Gradually people from older generations also got involved. It was a solidly working-class group.
>
> We would write, read and discuss what we'd written – mostly poems or stories – and occasionally we would have an outside guest come along. I particularly remember Adrian Mitchell, whose work I very much admired and enjoyed. But it was not an exercise in navel-gazing. We were into making writing a public thing. And this was at a time, remember, when I don't think there was a single bookshop in the whole borough of Tower Hamlets.
>
> Through the Basement Writers we learned how to turn words into action. We wrote, designed, pasted up, sold and flyposted a series of poetry posters. We self-published a series of poetry pamphlets. Alan Gilbey wrote and drew a prescient comic about the redevelopment of Docklands, which was turned into a musical show that we performed during the local E1 Festival. We organised a series of public poetry readings at the Half Moon Theatre, then in Aldgate. I can recall (retired) dockers' leader Jack Dash turning up and reading his poems at one of these events. Veterans of the anti-fascist Battle of Cable Street also took part. As did our founder Chris Searle, and his jazz-poetry group Two Fingers (there were three of them).
>
> A group of us from Sir John Cass took to visiting the poet Stephen Hicks at his Stepney home near our school. He was a pensioner and was in poor health, but his amusing and sometimes poignant verse always went down well at our poetry readings. A former boxer – under the name Johnny Hicks – it seemed to brighten up his day to have a few teenagers turning up to ask him about the old days and to laugh at his poems.
>
> The Basement Writers was probably unusual in spanning the generations in this way. And as a writers' group I think it was unusual in being

quite so involved in organising things and taking literature out to the public through posters, readings, shows, 'stunts' at festivals, going on radio, sending poems into local newspapers, and so on. We even had our own banner that was taken on the occasional demonstration.

There was some good writing in amongst it all, but you wouldn't want to spend the rest of your life reading only the stuff we produced. That wasn't the point.

The point was that we discovered that literature could be enjoyed; that literature could also be produced; that literature could concern our own lives and communities; and that we could be producers and organisers instead of just consumers. Had it been three years later we'd probably have started a DIY punk band instead!

It wasn't total revelation, because I had already developed an interest in politics and literature before the Basement Writers had formed. And two of us had published an unofficial school magazine. But the Basement certainly gave us the confidence, the experience and the contacts to extend such activities beyond our previous imaginations.

And, in one way or another, some of us have been earning our livings by writing ever since.[20]

Notes

1 Chris Searle (ed.), *Elders*, Reality Press, London, 1972.
2 Stephen Hicks, *The Boxer Speaks*, The Basement Writers, London, 1973.
3 Chris Searle, op. cit.
4 Stephen Hicks, *Sparring for Luck*, THAP Publishing, London, 1982.
5 Tony Harcup, *Never Had it So Good*, The Basement Writers, London, 1973.
6 Stephen Hicks, op. cit.
7 Leslie Mildiner and Bill House, *The Gates*, Centerprise, London, 1974.
8 Jim Wolveridge, *Aint it Grand*? Stepney Books, London, 1976.
9 Robert Barltrop and Jim Wolveridge, *The Muvver Tongue*, Journeyman Press, London, 1980.
10 'Poetry Poster', The Basement Writers, London, 1973.
11 'Second Poetry Poster', The Basement Writers, London, 1974.
12 Peter Blackman, *My Song is For All Men*, Lawrence & Wishart, London, 1952.
13 Gladys McGee, *Breaking Through*, The Basement Writers, London, 1975.
14 Gladys McGee, *Empire Day: 48 Great Poems*, a tape by Easytime Limited, London, (undated).
15 Sally Flood, *Window on Brick Lane*, The Basement Writers, London, 1979.
16 From *XX Years in the Basement*, The Basement Writers, London, 1993.
17 Debbie Carnegie, *Bedwritten*, The Basement Writers, London, 1974.
18 Alan Gilbey, *Up the Docks*, The Basement Writers, London, 1974.
19 *XX Years in the Basement*, op. cit.
20 From a letter to the author, 28 July 1997.

5

CLASSROOMS OF RESISTANCE

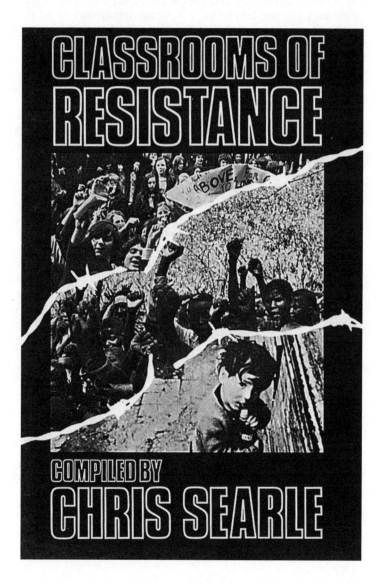

If some hostile spirits greeted the publication and purpose of *Ferndale Fires*, they were very muted compared to the reception of *Classrooms of Resistance*,[1] published in 1976 and composed of work done with Sir John Cass students after my eventual return to the school. Published by the Writers and Readers Cooperative, with the express purpose of reaching teachers nationally, as well as the students and their communities locally, it sought to demonstrate some aspects of the process and content of teaching 'English' to secondary-school students, using a body of knowledge ranging from the local response to the commercial redevelopment of docklands and the loss of local housing, the closure of a local hospital, the experiences of work and the struggle of Ford car workers, miners, building workers, and women workers in a local metal box factory. It sought to internationalize issues such as the Carletonville massacre and anti-apartheid resistance in South Africa, the coup in Chile, and the repression of Catholic schoolchildren by British soldiers in Belfast. Its primary intention was as a curriculum challenge, to demonstrate that given the classroom opportunity, inner-city pupils would respond positively, and with a high sense of motivation and enthusiasm, towards knowledge and curriculum that directly affected themselves, their communities and other working-class communities and struggling people all over the world.

Even before it was officially published, the pink pages of the *Financial Times* ran a large feature on the book, stretching across an entire page under the headline 'Teaching Revolution in the Classroom'.[2] Whereas the establishment press had, often reluctantly, been prepared to accept the validity of *Stepney Words* where the poetry had often been marked by a sense of alienation, where the protest of the words had been individualistic and sometimes desolate, the work in *Classrooms of Resistance* was much more combative and marked by a collective sense of students working together, sharing similar insights and combining to write playlets and dramatic sketches. The theme of 'loneliness' had moved on to that of 'union' and many of the writers expressed their words not as if they were 'losing', but as if the opportunity of winning through against conditions around them was real and viable. Thus, in *Stepney Words*, the introductory poem was by a 12-year-old boy who had written these few anonymous words on an otherwise bare sheet left on a desk:

> I am just a boy
>   with a lot of dreams
> but what's the point
>   I won't get nowhere
> I'm just ordinary
>   nothing special just
>   ... ordinary
> got no chance in this
>   world unless you're
>   ... clever
> which I'm not[3]

In *Classrooms of Resistance* another 12-year-old wrote about the closure of her local hospital with these words:

Poplar Hospital

81 beds going to waste
That is not enough in this place.
To the government that's their way
To let the people die on the street
And on a windy day.
But if they are ill
They have their private wards
    so that they get well.
They must say:
'Let them die in Poplar,
    we are okay,
In our private wards
    living like lords
Every day.'

Beverly

And a girl classmate wrote about the building of a luxury hotel (the Tower Hotel) in derelict docklands near the decaying block of flats where she lived:

Houses for People

What is to be done
With this land that is left?
Will there be at last
Nice houses for people to rest?
Why don't we build houses
So clean, neat and bright
Instead of these shabby things
People dwell in day and night.

This new place they have built
Called the Tower Hotel, is not for us,
But for rich people to dwell,
And with what land there is left
They want to build more,
All for the rich
None for the poor.

We will fight to stop them building,
And we'll build just what we like –
Just for the less rich people
We will make a happy sight.

> And if they try to stop us
> We will fight and not give in,
> Until we get our houses built
> We will fight until we win.
>
> *Kym*

There was a marked difference between the tone of the two sets of poems, and it was precisely that change that the establishment commentators recognized, and in the main, did not like. There was no longer a note of resignation or acceptance in the poems, something, it seemed, that worried the press guardians of 'liberal democracy'. In the *Financial Times*, Joe Rogaly wrote:

> What does the liberal democracy say at this stage? Again the answer is not clear. Many of the individual pieces in *Classrooms of Resistance*, taken alone, should not be suppressed or used as a cause for preventing Mr. Searle from teaching in any society with pretensions to be free.
>
> Yet he does not himself seem to have changed his mind about the best approach to teaching. He feels he is part of a movement of young teachers like himself, who believe that the classroom is, in his words, 'a place to develop collective consciousness and action, and to transform education into the will to resist and organise'.

And he concluded his article with this sentence:

> If the present danger to democracy in Britain is not to become over-whelming, we must first make up our minds about where this line is to be drawn, and then cast aside inhibitions in defending it.

The writer was incorrect on one very specific point. I had moved on in the sense that I had become much more emphatic about the *content* of my teaching. While still taking a teaching approach that was 'situational' and pitching my classroom work firstly in the immediate neighbourhood world of the students, then in the workplaces where they might well be headed, and then moving to internationalist contexts like South Africa, Chile and Ireland, I was more determined to deal with *dynamic* situations where struggle and change were in progress. Thus, instead of the general issue of the plight of the old in East London, I moved to the specific situation of resistance to the closure of the local hospital they might be using; instead of the general topic of poor housing and unheated flats, I turned to the local campaign to secure new housing for local people on the derelict land of the London docklands which was becoming a speculator's paradise; instead of general poetic statements about racism and the plight of black communities, I shifted to resistance to apartheid in South Africa, and the life of the eighteenth-century Jewish boxer, Daniel Mendoza, whose career had been a long fight against racism before he became the champion of all England. His struggle was used as a source of emulation for Bengali students facing violent racism on the streets of East London in the early 1970s. In short, the contextual work became more specific and more allied to situations of resistance and struggle.

There was the same lyricism, witty use of words and rhyming humour in *Classrooms of Resistance* as there had been in *Stepney Words*, such as in this 12-year-old boy's poem about the maritime Wapping of his dockland family's memory, a place that was passing:

Wapping

Wapping is nice
    and you can smell
that spice,
Big ships
    small ships
        all kinds of ships.
Little sparrows
    flying like arrows
through the air
        landing nowhere.

Sailors have mynah birds
    shouting out dirty words
That's what it's like in
    Wapping.

Peter

And the loneliness of single people became the loneliness and desperation of an entire oppressed people, overrun by their rulers' brutal and fascist army:

The flag of Chile represents
The blood of death,
The star is the star of freedom,
The white is the emptiness of lonely people

Frances

The same *Financial Times* and its pink pages would print much, of course, over the next few years, praising the progress of Chile's new 'model' economy.

'There is no doubt that *Classrooms of Resistance* is clear indoctrination,' declared the *Daily Telegraph*:[4] 'Nowhere throughout the 168 pages is there the faintest ray of pleasure or the innocence of a child's humour'. Where was the cockney sparrow? (Apart from those flying like arrows off the deserted Wapping Docks). But these are not poems, stories and dramatic sketches of innocence. The pleasure being derived by the writers is the pleasure of empathy – sharing the satisfaction of a Ford worker outwitting his management, the sense of victory of a group of women factory workers knowing they have won their strike, of a branch of building workers proudly picketing, knowing that 'even Uri Geller cannot break our wall of steel!' Or John Fontaine's exhilarating 'sit in' in the cabin of a giant crane, high up in the sky. In these pieces the underdogs refuse to be losers, they rise up and fight back. So that must be 'indoctrination' or, in the words of the reviewer of *Classrooms of Resistance* in the *Times Educational Supplement*, such children can only be 'mindless replicators'.[5] For to demonstrate that working-class young people can understand the logic and empathy of winning through, that they need not be mindless and simple *un*conscious reproducers and copycats of the teachers' diktat must be to demonstrate a process of 'indoctrination'. Just like it was 'indoctrination' when the 800 Stepney children organized, stewarded, publicized and skilfully conducted their own strike outside the gates of their school. So many times over the last 30 years have I heard this spurious argument: 'children can't organize anything, can't create any event' unless there is an adult, a 'Pied Piper' like myself leading and manipulating them.

But the most manic comments about *Classrooms of Resistance* were by the columnist Peregrine Worsthorne, also deputy editor of the *Sunday Telegraph*. 'Get Class out of the Classroom!'[6] his article was headlined, and if there were any further proof needed that the teacher who applies creative pedagogy and critical literacy in the classroom is going to be besieged by hostility, obsessive anger and a furious antipathy, then it is to be found in the rabid words of this piece of polemic journalism, which ended by calling for my removal from teaching (as had the review in the *Daily Telegraph*) in this fashion: 'The sooner he is sacked, "pour encourager les autres" – of whom there are far too many – the better'.

Of course, Worsthorne was masquerading as the defender of working-class children, protecting them from a teacher who was offering 'a degree of intellectual meanness, not to say sadism, far more outrageous and unforgivable than the worst excesses of Mr. Squeers'.

To read these fulminations, spread over five columns of print adjacent to the paper's leader column, surprised even my sensitivity, which by this time had become accustomed to such diatribes. They reminded me again of just what exactly lay behind the façade of 'liberal democracy' of the British education system, and how fragile it was. I had, by this time, been introduced to the work of Paulo Freire, and I was well aware that his imprisonment and exile had followed the Brazilian military coup in 1964. Ironically, after publishing five articles over two issues that violently attacked *Classrooms of Resistance*, the *Time Educational Supplement* in its leader column included a short political digest which suggested that the writer too knew very well what was at stake with the coordinated assault on the book:

> Mr. Searle is a lively and combative exponent of an approach to education which bears a close resemblance to that of Paulo Freire, the Brazilian philosopher and adult educator, who argues that the key to learning is to be found in giving the learner insight into the social, economic and political realities which dominate his existence. It is Marxist in its assumption that the ownership of the means of production, distribution

and exchange determine the consciousness of children in school, and their families. Hence, opening their eyes to a Marxist analysis of the distribution of power within society, is the first step on the road to learning.

The motive force for education, according to this view, is found in the desire to change the society by radical criticism and action: this is the guiding light which can generate an effective desire to learn in children who otherwise are likely to feel helpless and impotent.[7]

Considering its source, this was strangely well put, and at odds with the declared view of one of *Classrooms of Resistance*'s castigators in two previous issues, Professor of Education John Vaizey, who had pledged:

It is not now, and never has been, the primary purpose of our education system to indoctrinate children into political or class beliefs. It is certainly true that the 'hidden curriculum' may have such effects, though the evidence is less clear ... The point is, however, that there is all the difference in the world between openly seeking to do something and a more subtle and unconscious form of indoctrination.[8]

The crime of *Classrooms of Resistance* then, was to *openly* propose that education and its foundation, literacy, should be an instrument for transforming the lives of young people of the working class: that was its temerity, its outright cheek. Certainly the 'radical criticism and action' recognized by the *Times Educational Supplement*'s leader had overcome a sense of passivity and even feelings of being 'helpless and impotent' emerging from some of the *Stepney Words* poetry (although not in the action to protest against its attempted suppression). Now *Classrooms of Resistance* was publishing the work of 11-year-old students who had the confidence to walk into the new Tower Hotel and ask for the tariff in order to bring it into their English classroom to examine it, and then write these lines about the new hotel and the huge construction company that built it:

Rich Luxuries

Why did Taylor Walker build the hotel?
When there are so many people who have
    nowhere to dwell?
The Tower Hotel is only for millionaires
There is nowhere for us to live or to play.
In the Tower Hotel they have waitresses
Where we have to slave for ourselves,
They have luxuries galore
Our homes are just a bore
They have 836 rooms in the hotel
Where we are scrambled up in about four.

Lynn

Such young women were clearly not 'helpless and impotent' – critical learning was coming to the centre of their lives and confidence. The ubiquitous 'they' who controlled their lives was being named, identified, whether it was Taylor Walker, the giant Strand Group of hotels, or the East Metropolitan Regional Hospital Board that was closing down the local hospital:

Poplar Hospital

Poplar Hospital is closing down
And people start to gather round,
Screaming, shouting, waving banners
And saying that they will be the
                                winners.

They say it is understaffed
But the nurses say 'that's a laugh!'
They lie and cheat the public so
They say the East Metropolitan Regional
                    Board should go.
All those beds lie empty now,
Why, some half-dead person could be cured.
So people, people, come out and support us
Or that dead person could be you!

Sharon, 13

Words were becoming names, pronouns were becoming proper nouns and there was a dimension of discovery here for the young writers, an opening up of understanding that was bringing some discomfort to the established interests of education and beyond.

At least all the kerfuffle and reaction to *Classrooms of Resistance* also provoked the opportunity for me to put my own case within the *Times Educational Supplement*.[9] It was published under the appropriate title of 'All in the Same Class' (for which I thank the sub-editor!) and I will quote it in full because I think it best explains why *Classrooms of Resistance* was compiled, and the thought behind the practice that it sought to document:

An established educational maxim, purveyed through training colleges and educational authorities, upheld by 'educationists' (I have often wondered what they are, if they are not working teachers) and often insisted on by headteachers, is that teachers' attitudes to the body of knowledge they transmit to their pupils is impartial.

The teacher is seen as the pilot of an unbiased passage of facts through the uncommitted atmosphere of the classroom, into the minds of children, who are receptive if they are middle class, but resistant if they are working class. This notion is vindicated as being the most objective and fair. The teacher takes the chair between the syllabus on the one hand and the children's minds on the other.

More than ever, these hypocritical and shallow dogmas are being challenged by classroom teachers throughout the country, particularly in the urban working-class areas, where in every area of public service – through housing, law, unemployment, health, physical environment and education – people face systematic underdevelopment and attack. Educational resources are axed, hospitals are closed, local councils allot the few new council flats available to young couples through a Bingo system, and traditional industrial areas are robbed of employment by the owners of wealth moving their industry to areas which offer cheaper rates and labour.

The schools are pitched in the centre of this battlefield. From my classroom, my class and I overlook vast, dying dockyards and vacant building lots waiting for houses. Up the road to the east of the borough, Poplar Hospital is closing down; to the west towards the Tower of London, the Tower Hotel opens in the dockyards of St Katherine's Docks, with penthouse suites at £54 a night; the basin is filled with luxury yachts, making a new international marina. Warehouses and riverside houses have been converted into elegant studio flats for those with the necessary wealth to buy them. Many of our children and their families still wait to be rehoused from appalling conditions.

Individually, and sometimes as entire staffs, teachers have always fought against these local injustices by bringing them into the classroom. They have abandoned a neutrality of viewpoint which necessarily vindicates their continuation. They urge their children, through committed teaching and a committed syllabus, to also come out of school fighting and campaigning to redress these wrongs and inequalities. They have urged, although they might not have expressed it in such a way, a certain thinking power or consciousness – an ideology of resistance.

An immeasurable development is when those teachers become organized, within their union or their staffroom, with a collective viewpoint which upholds and supports that ideology. Then the kind of minority resistance to school which the establishment press joys to publicize and savour, the teacher-bashing, the claims of falls in standards, the supposed comprehensive chaos, become transformed into the collective resistance of the classroom, where teacher and children together make a workshop of struggle where a new consciousness and new intention is born.

Classrooms of Resistance is only one indication of this movement among teachers. The book could have been made of work between teachers and their pupils in almost any area of any one of our cities, so much similar committed and creative effort is being generated from British classrooms. Whereas the capitalist media emphasize truancy among working-class children, with a relish which persuades us they are by no means unpleased to see it happen, this book emphasizes utter commitment to the classroom, not as a place to be bored or alienated, but as a place to develop collective consciousness and action and to transform education into the will to resist and organize.

In working towards this, the collective action of teachers, unionized and organizing together at their place of work, has a chance to partially transform the school as a salient that can make a huge dent in the line of capitalist continuity, and promote a future breakthrough. With a syllabus designed not to trample the children's inevitable resistance, but to engage it and marry it with the teachers' own commitment to change society, the school can be overturned from within as an agency of capitalist society which has promoted and perpetuated the conflicting relationships between its workforces.

When teachers are told of their need to be the impartial observers of the classroom, they are effectively instructed to exclude political opinion and commitment from their teaching. They are told that this enables them to be objective and promotes an impartial passage of facts. Certainly *Classrooms of Resistance* was compiled out of a need to be objective. It is a perfectly objective truth that, for example, unemployment for school leavers is approaching 20 per cent in the London Borough of Tower Hamlets; that land speculation and profiteering on a vast scale has begun with the building of the Tower Hotel, and is planned to continue with the growing re-development of London dockland; that Poplar Hospital is scheduled to be closed.

What is false is the notion that true objectivity can exist in or control a classroom without a political perspective. Teachers themselves know these facts as they teach, as they also know how they affect their livelihood in a period of teacher redundancy, when their own union locally is trying to save the jobs of other teachers who have been dismissed through education cuts. The potential unemployment of their own pupils and the risks of their own redundancy are implacably linked through the political reality they both move within and share, working together in the classroom. This in itself makes for an elision of consciousness which is both entirely objective and entirely political, completely removed from the bogus objectivity argued by the educational hierarchs. Thus a new empathy is forged between the teacher and the pupil who work together – they are in, and of, the same class.

The teacher and child, working towards this comradeship of the classroom, created in spite of the terrible gulf the bourgeois school imposes between the teacher and the working-class child, look around them. For either of them, John Berger's words have real truth: 'He lives in the contradiction between what he is and what he would like to be. Either he then becomes fully conscious of the contradiction and its causes, and so joins the political struggle for a full democracy which entails, among other things, the overthrow of capitalism; or else he lives, continually subject to an envy which, compounded with his sense of powerlessness, dissolves into recurrent daydreams'.

Certainly, *Classrooms of Resistance* is a compilation that avoids daydreams and fantasy. Through their individual imaginations set at work through classroom stimulation, children empathize and collectivize with the people of Chile and South Africa, the youth of Belfast, striking women in a local metal box factory, Yorkshire miners, Shrewsbury building workers. They also consider local attacks on themselves and their families through the dockland speculation and the closing of Poplar Hospital.

The book has been assembled using many photographs supporting the work of the children, providing visual reinforcement to their imaginations. The work can then be seen out of its classroom context, as the objective truth of the world. The children, like all British working-class children, are an extension of the children of Chile, South Africa or Belfast: their class unites them and their poetry brings solidarity with them, and urges them, through a process of imaginative empathy, to share both their oppression and resistance.

There was a strong response to this article, with letters and further articles being published in subsequent issues of the *Times Educational Supplement*. The most persistent theme was the argument over 'English' teaching and individualism: 'Children are, and must be left as individuals', wrote F.W. Edwards of Gwent.[10] 'A humane society arises through its own constructive efforts. The informed, questioning mind is education's highest product – a dalek-like monotype from Chile to Langdon Park [*the name of the school I had joined in 1974*] is not. There is possibly a good case for the closing of the Poplar Hospital based on helping people more. It is arguable that a society which put the Tower Hotel in place of tenement flats is offering a higher standard of living to more and more.' I had no disagreement with the writer's first two statements – I subscribed in principle to them. But then the question of alternative content and genuine critical perspectives arises. His argument suggested that the perspectives being handed to the local community were the absolute truth: the process we were involved with in the classroom was precisely to critically examine them and search under their surfaces. It was that process through language and the imagination that was provoking the attack. Mr Edwards' assertion was that 'social conscience' in teaching 'needs to develop and gain a balancing condition': *Classrooms of Resistance* was calling for new scales of knowledge, curriculum and pedagogy which were not weighted against the working-class learner, which enabled the truth of social conditions to be told and from that, the cultural action to be developed and encouraged – in the context of the opportunity to *gain* and *win* a betterment of life.

We had seen enough of working-class children losing, and this being a constantly-evoked theme in their writing. As I wrote in my letter of response to the attacks made upon *Classrooms of Resistance* in the *Times Educational Supplement* (particularly the review by Geoffrey Summerfield):

I am very sorry that *Classrooms of Resistance* stuck in Geoffrey Summerfield's throat, and I hope that it does not stop his *Voices*, which I have often used in the classroom. Mr. Summerfield likes those 'poignant and vivid' pieces which show working-class children as losers. His satisfaction with a story in *Classrooms of Resistance* in which a boy tells of the death of his dog reflects the general praise for the similarly eloquent *Kes*.

As long as English lessons deal with the poignancy and despair of working-class children experiencing and expressing a sense of loss or deprivation – whether it is dog, kestrel, the right to work, a decent house, a fulfilled life – then the English work is deemed satisfying. When the children are on the offensive, discovering and articulating the injustice which surrounds them and so often smothers them and makes them losers, and combining with the teacher in the classroom to begin through language, imagination and empathy to work against and triumph over these injustices, then even people like Mr. Summerfield choose to leave themselves behind as if they are afraid of working-class children ever losing that sense of loss and despair which moves them so much. As a man who has contributed much to English teaching, he should be with us and those children he has sought to reach with his work.[11]

More of Geoffrey Summerfield in a subsequent chapter, but *Classrooms of Resistance* had its strong advocates too, beyond the students and their families who spoke up for it. Since such a vital part of the compilation was concerned with what was happening in the London docklands, *Socialist Worker* decided to give it to an active trade-unionist docker to review.[12] He wrote:

Classrooms of Resistance is the follow-up to *Stepney Words*. What interests me, as someone brought up in East London (where, as in most working-class areas, school is boring and a place you rush to get away from) is how ... children, who would ordinarily be written off as no-hopers, produce work of the highest quality. Not surprisingly, the response of the children is to identify completely with their sisters and brothers from other lands.

Can you imagine the impact of dissatisfied, articulate working-class children with a belief in their ability to change things, working in the factories, the mines, the docks? This book confirms what many have always known, working-class children, given the right kind of challenge and leadership, will respond. They will produce imaginative work and actions which augur well in the struggle for a future socialist Britain.

And he finished with a rhetorical question to the notorious adherent of 'genetic' politics and 'race science': 'Are you listening, Dr. Eysenck?'

His review was a published version of the themes of many letters that I had received during the heat after the publication of *Classrooms of Resistance*, some from teachers, but others from people who, in the past, had gone to school in East London. After a television news programme where the book had been discussed by Rhodes Boyson, an ex-headteacher and now Conservative MP, and myself, in which Boyson had launched into a diatribe and labelled me a 'Pied Piper', I received a number of letters of solidarity. In one of these, the correspondent wrote:

In the 1930s I used to attend Red Coat School at the the top of Garden Street, Stepney. Our family were very poor in those days. The teachers

at the school seemed only interested in conning us, not trying to edu-
cate us. I enjoyed listening to you on the television last night, I only
wish that we had had teachers like you. Please carry on your good work
for working-class children.

Such messages of encouragement were not uncommon from those who
had been through the system and emerged with insight from its other end.
Another interested viewer wrote:

> If by your teaching children are enabled to overthrow *anything* at all that
> oppresses them; if by your teaching, they are suitably prepared for the
> life they are going to live; if by your teaching, they will have a voice
> loud enough to be heard in the world, then good luck to them! You
> don't indoctrinate children – you don't have to! You merely supply
> them with the tools and opportunities which they are going to be able to
> put to use in life, and which those better off than they have always had.

This understanding of *class* in education, and a system of education which
expressed and reproduced it, was, of course, behind all the passionate argument and fear that was raised by the publication of *Classrooms of Resistance*.
Critical literacy in the inner-city context opens young people's eyes not
so much to the reality of class, for they already have that understanding
in their very bones, but to the possibilities of action and change that follow such an understanding. And that is what fired up the defenders and
advantage-takers of the established system. During the *Stepney Words* strike,
the hundreds of students had found new words to a football chant they
all knew, and hurled them at the cause of their grievance across East London
in a huge unison:

> We hate the Governors,
> Oh yes we do!
> We hate the Governors
> Oh yes we do![13]

'The Governors' or 'Guv'nors': Londonese for the bosses, the controllers, the
rulers, the suppressors, the oppressors. Now that same sense of grievance and
campaigning energy was being transformed and was now coming out through
those writing in their classrooms and using their imaginations to extend
themselves to the factories where their mothers worked, or where they might
work themselves in the all-too-close future:

> **Pay Us!**
>
> Workers today don't get enough
> In some cases they have strikes –
> Roads with banners they have walked
> > day and night,

Keeping fighting.
Even they have wrote to Parliament,
Rowing for more payment.
So Governors, give us more money!

Likely we will strike to this day,
If I were you, I'd give in,
For you don't stand a chance.
End this strike and pay us!

Tracy

Fortunately, for a much more insightful interpretation of the purpose of *Classrooms of Resistance*, the books editor of *New Society* invited John Berger to write a review. Berger, Booker Prize winner and one of Britain's leading novelists and cultural critics, understood immediately this theme of *class*:

Chris Searle teaches English in a London East End secondary school. His pupils are working class. Around the school the docks are being closed down, social services are being cut, unemployment is increasing and the poverty of the permitted choices is becoming more and more obvious. Nearby, a luxury hotel of over 800 rooms, has been built, warehouses are being transformed into expensive flats and a mooring 'port' has been opened for private yachts. All this outside the classroom. Inside, what should the kids be studying and writing about? Wordsworth, A Walk in the Country, My Favourite TV Programme?

Searle allows them to think and feel about what is happening *outside* the classroom and what is likely to happen next – given who they are. I say *allow*, because if not discouraged, it is what they might begin to do for themselves. I say *given who they are* because the first principle of his lessons is self-recognition. All the kids have been born into an exploited class. If they don't resist they will be worse-paid and worse-housed. By encouraging such self-recognition, a sense of justice and the will to fight back, his English lessons arm the adolescents for the lives already allotted to them as adults by a class society.

Searle's example reveals something which the ruling class does not want revealed. In a class society there is no such thing as education as a universal right. The state educational system has two main functions: to train 'streams' of a labour force so that they can passively perform the different necessary jobs, and beyond that, to preserve ignorance. Searle, by teaching his pupils what they need to know for their own interest (in both senses of the word), opposes both functions. Not surprisingly there- fore, *Classrooms of Resistance* has provoked wild protests in the establish- ment press.

At the height of the Church's power every unwelcome recognition of reality was condemned as heresy; today every unwelcome truth is condemned as *propaganda*. When it is a truth which, once stated, is self-evident, it is called extremist propaganda. And so Searle is labelled a propagandist among our innocent young. A political pied piper! In fact, like all inspiring teachers accused of subversion, he simply suggests that his pupils connect together what they already know. And before anything else, these kids know what is being done to them and their brothers and fathers and mothers.[14]

When I read these words I thanked the writer in my head and my heart a million times. I had wanted to find the words myself, but he had found them for me. I experienced the same sense of recognition that he attributed to my own students; for that was at the core of a knowledge that continued on and developed into action, into protest and resistance against that very type of society built upon classes that he was explaining so solidly and with so much clarity – just as my students did, with, in the words of Swift, who knew the same things himself 'simple words in simple places'. Berger went on to explain the particular skill and achievement that the students showed, which had been missed, misinterpreted and rejected by the squad of establishment voices and the lords of education that had assailed their work:

A few of the poems and stories – like the story of a green jacket by Mahbubur Rahman – display impressive literary talent. But the talent which most of them display is of another kind. The talent, the faculty of imaginative empathy. They prove Adam Smith and Ricardo and Mill wrong: egoism is not the first motive of man. Solidarity is deeper and more natural.

They also refute the great philistine petit bourgeois pragmatic edict, born of a fear of the imagination, that you yourself have to experience a thing before you can say anything about it. On the contrary, the authors of this book know that all imagination begins with the ability to identify with the experience of others, who are like yourself but different.

This book is a gift for anybody, although it derives from and is marked by tragedy.

It is a deeply moving and affirmative experience to have such a powerful writer describing the work of your students with such insight. It is even more so when the students themselves back you up and defend your pedagogy. The response to *Stepney Words* had proved this to me, but *Classrooms of Resistance* had provoked even more potent enemies and forces to show their power. In that context, any hostility or its reinforcement from my students or their families could have finished me as a teacher in a state school. By the time of the publication of *Classrooms of Resistance* I had moved to a neighbouring school, where I was offered more responsibility, without the stigma and victimization from the school management that I had found when I returned to teach at Sir John Cass for another year from 1973 to 1974. *Classrooms of Resistance* was published in 1976, and newspapers like the *Daily Mail* (which had supported Hitler in the 1930s) accused me in their editorials of 'lurching from teaching towards indoctrination' and encouraging my students to 'worship at the shrines of Communist martyrs like Allende and to look up to the Shrewsbury Two and see class conflict in every situation from Ulster to overcrowding in hospital wards'.[15] The London *Evening Standard* quoted Rhodes Boyson MP as saying 'He is preparing children for bovver boots, leather jackets and thuggery – it's sheer indoctrination'.[16] It was an open incitement to my students and their families to hound me out of teaching. But the opposite happened. The students again stood up for me. When the tabloid journalists came down to the school gates with their orders to find juice, scandal and defamity about this particular teacher, they found loyalty and solidarity and nothing which they could use to condemn me. As the *Evening Standard* reported – and I cite these words not through egoism, but through a wish to show the steadfastness and support of these students:

> Pupils in Mr. Searle's class at Langdon Park Comprehensive School, Poplar, have leapt to his defence.
> John Smith, 13 said: 'We are very lucky to have him. He makes sure we are well-educated. He just teaches us what our rights are.'
> The boys said they were free to have their own ideas in class.
> 'I often disagree with him,' said Jimmy Doyle: 'I don't believe there should be strikes, for instance, and he says we should always make up our own minds.'
> Steven Mason, 13 said: 'Mr. Searle is the best teacher in the school. He encourages us to argue back at him.' Harry Curtin 13, said: 'He insists on good behaviour and proper punctuation and things like that.'[17]

In 30 years of teaching, and often going from predicament to predicament, sometimes in very vulnerable curcumstances, I have never been exposed or let down by my students. Perhaps I have sometimes been lucky, but I prefer to see it in terms of that word which my critics and detractors have always scorned – solidarity. And what is this word 'solidarity'? What does it mean? I would prefer its definition to be marked by the words of one of my students, who wrote these lines which I used as the watchwords and preface to *Classrooms of Resistance*:

> But love is more than a metaphor
> it's a sledgehammer to break down doors.
> It's an axe to free the chained.
> Free each other, work for each other,
> > Love each other
> > enough to feel each other's pain.
>
> *Tony Harcup*

Notes

1 Chris Searle, *Classrooms of Resistance*, Writers and Readers Cooperative, London, 1975.
2 *Financial Times*, 14 October 1975.

3 *Stepney Words*, Reality Press, London, 1971.
4 *Daily Telegraph*, 29 January 1976.
5 *Times Educational Supplement*, 31 October 1975.
6 *Sunday Telegraph*, 19 October 1975.
7 *Times Educational Supplement*, 14 November 1975.
8 *Times Educational Supplement*, 31 October 1975.
9 *Times Educational Supplement*, 10 October 1975.
10 *Times Educational Supplement*, op. cit.
11 *Times Educational Supplement*, 31 October 1975.
12 *Socialist Worker*, 17 January 1976.
13 See Chris Searle, *This New Season*, Calder & Boyars, London, 1973.
14 *New Society*, 27 November 1975.
15 *Daily Mail*, 15 October 1975.
16 *Evening Standard*, 24 October 1975.
17 *Evening Standard*, ibid.

6

THE PEOPLE
MARCHING ON

Photograph © Ron McCormick

The radical American educationist Peter McLaren asks in his book *Critical Pedagogy and Predatory Culture*: 'How can students engage history as a way of reclaiming power and identity?'[1] A powerful and essential question this, and one certainly worth the search and struggle to answer. Our students were living and studying within the landscape of a dramatic and decisive history. East London had been the birthplace of modern trade unionism, of titanic struggles of ordinary working people, of insurgent women and their early movements for improved conditions of work, for the vote and human dignity. It had been the venue of mass movements against fascism and racism in solidarity with the progress of struggling peoples in other lands. All this activity of history had thrown up outstanding leaders and exemplars of courage, ingenuity and creative skill. And yet little of this was in the history books that the students were told to study. It was still a history of kings and queens, generals and battles, churchmen and imperialists. History had been lived in the very streets around the school. A student called Harry Tillett was the great-grandson of the man who led the great dockers' strike of 1889. Within the historical memories of our students' families were events of profound significance and people's resistance, blocked out of the history to be 'officially' compartmentalized, categorized and 'delivered' in schools. The other history, this popular history of class, families and communities needed to be rediscovered, revived and rekindled in the minds and imaginations of new generations as a source of pride, truth and emulation.

A main section of my book *The World in a Classroom* (1977)[2] describes what I called 'the embrace of history' in the English and literacy classes at Langdon Park School, Poplar, during the years 1974–6. The result of much of this teaching was also published in a book, printed and published locally, which we called *The People Marching On*[3] (from a line in William Morris' poem 'The March of the Workers'). Below the title was printed: 'Written and re-lived by the Second and Third year children of Langdon Park School, Poplar, London E14, 1974–5'. The use of the word 're-lived' was vital, for the objective of the teaching was to dispense with the barriers between subjects like 'English' and 'history', and working with an integral vision, encourage our students through the power of their imaginative empathy and historical memory to re-engage with the past and live its drama, tragedy and progress alongside their own grandparents and forebears. The determined women and men who organized the matchgirls' strike at the Bryant and May factory at Bow in 1888, the dockers, gasworkers, transport workers, the East London suffragettes, the anti-fascists who repulsed Mosley's Blackshirts in Cable Street in 1936 – they did not worry whether knowledge was 'English', 'history', 'literature' or 'sociology': knowing was organic, connected to action and struggle for the betterment of their families' lives. There were no spurious categories: literacy was there to serve a movement of people who had been denied justice and the most elementary benefits of a decent life.

The prime curriculum materials were there to be uncovered in the files and shelves of the local history rooms of the nearby central borough library, on the microfilms of local newspapers going back to the mid nineteenth century. As teachers we also became researchers, as this was a collective effort, involving five teachers committed to the project. We found autobiographies and memoirs of the leaders and the rank and file of those men and women involved in these events, and we unearthed their songs and poems, most of which had not been read since the time of their original publication in journals and broadsheets. In the *Women's Dreadnaught*, the journal of the East London Federation of Suffragettes, we found this startling lyric, a mock-lullaby:

> O hush thee my baby, thy sire was a slave,
> Whom overwork thrust in the dark early grave;
> The gloomy, grey streets from this den which we see,
> Are hungrily waiting, dear baby for thee,
> O hush thee my baby.
>
> O sleep whilst thou may, babe, by night and by day
> Thy pale mother rests not, but stitches away;
> There's no one to guard thee from hunger but she,
> Her tears flowing silently all for thee,
> O hush thee my baby.
>
> O hush thee my baby through days dark and wild
> Stream sun-shafts of glory that can't be defiled;
> The marching of myriads is borne to our ears,
> And we will march with them, and sing through our tears,
> O hush thee my baby.[4]

There was the moving anonymous poem 'On the Stones', taken from an issue of the *East End News* in 1889, at the time of the great docks strike. The first verse wondered:

> How many thousands do not know
> The hardships of a docker's life;
> What hours and days he has to wait
> For work to keep his home and wife.
> Oft' days and weeks he strives to hear
> The ganger call the name he owns.
> How hard he struggles to the front;
> But still is left 'upon the stones.'

There were still more anonymous poems from long obscure local anthologies that described the area in word-pictures that searched for hope and release:

> And even in Canning Town, where no white tree
> Symbols the far-flung rapture of the Spring,
> Some dream of beauty by the wind is stirred
> Some envy of the careless birds that wing
> High o'er her smoke, some longing for a word
> To break her evil spell and set her free.[5]

We found songs, chants and ditties that accompanied strikes and marches, and were still wonderfully engaging to sing together, even in a classroom in Limehouse in 1975, like this 1889 dockers' song to the elusive 'sixpence':

> Sing a song of sixpence
> Dockers on the strike
> Guinea pigs as greedy
> As a hungry pike.
> Till docks are opened
> Burns for you will speak –
> Courage lads! And you'll win
> Well within the week!
> Norwood's in his counting house,
> Counting up his money,
> Says he finds his life now
> Isn't sweet as honey!
> Ships are in the river
> Lying there in rows –
> But the tardy tanner's coming
> Everybody Knows!

One of our team was a veteran colleague, a retired teacher now working part-time who remembered his experience as a schoolboy during the 1926 National Strike, and how he and his classmates all wore red ties to show their solidarity with the strikers. He told his story to the students, and wrote a poem for them to read and discuss. The curriculum was coming out of the teachers themselves, not only as scholars and researchers, but as poets and tellers too:

May 4th 1926

> May 4th 1926 – morning,
> East End classroom crowded
> With youth and feeling unconfined,
> Crimson ties proclaiming oneness
> With workers – red flags fluttering
> In the corridors of the mind.
> To bull-like masters red rags,
> Well-worn beyond these cock-crow years,
> Beyond betrayals and disasters;
> Remembrance that the battering shower
> Of time, its storms can never nip.
> Among her festivals and bitter tears
> Comes home this memory
> Like a well-laden, triumphant ship.

Bill Foot

We sent letters to parents for reminiscences, mementoes, documents and old press cuttings and newspapers. We were sent one extraordinary narrative poem about the October 1936 Battle of Cable Street on a broadsheet, by someone calling himself or herself 'The Tramp Poet' – an urban ancient mariner who buttonholes a passer-by and tells him with vivid images and dramatic incident the story of the defeat of the fascist Blackshirt march and the police who defended it.

The Battle of Cable Street

You ask me how I got like this, Sir,
Well I don't care to say,
But I will tell you a little story
Of when I was in a big fray.

I'm not very well in my old age,
And as I sits drinking my broth,
My mind goes back to 1936,
That Sunday, October the fourth.

I was walking down Bethnal Green Road, Sir,
Just walking about at my ease,
When the strains of a famous old song, Sir,
Came floating to me on the breeze.

I stopped, I looked and I listened,
Now where have I heard that old song?
Then I dashed to the Salmon and Ball, Sir
I knew I wouldn't go wrong.

It was the Internationale they were singing,
They were singing it with a defiant blast,
And holding up a big red banner
With these words: 'THEY SHALL NOT PASS'.

We then marched on to the East End,
We were five thousand of us, I am sure.
And when we got to the Aldgate,
We were met by three hundred thousand more.

'Red Front! Red Front!' these workers cried,
It was a sight I wouldn't have missed
To see these thousands of defiant workers
Holding up their mighty clenched fist.

The police said 'Now move along, please,
This is all we ask',

But we said 'No, not for those Blackshirts,
Those rotters, THEY SHALL NOT PASS'.

We then marched on to Stepney Green, Sir,
You could see that this fight was no sham,
For there were thousands of workers
Marching from Limehouse, Poplar, Stratford and East Ham.

You could see that Mosley wouldn't get through, Sir,
That our slogan that day was no boast,
And I shouted 'Hip, hip hurrah',
As I saw our flag being tied to a lamp-post.

The children shouted from the windows 'O, golly',
For Mosley no one seemed sorry,
But someone had had the goodness
To lend us their two-ton lorry.

We got it over on its side, Sir,
It wasn't much of a strain,
But the police kept knocking our barricade down
So we built the damn thing up again.

The police said we worked mighty fast
As with a hanky their faces they mopped,
So we got out our big red banner,
And stuck it right on the top.

The police then charged with their truncheons.
They charged us, the working class,
But they couldn't pinch our red banner
With these words 'THEY SHALL NOT PASS'.

I wish you had been there to see it,
You would have said it was a ruddy fine feat,
How we kept that old Red Flag flying
On those barricades of Cable Street.

So this is the end of my story
And I must get back to my broth,
But I hope you will never forget, Sir,
It was Sunday, October the fourth.

The Tramp Poet

This was a curriculum-in-the-making, and being made within the community of learners and their families – a process of building knowledge that was entirely organic, with back-to-the-source material which spoke of, affirmed and gave value and integrity to the people who studied it, and their families – unlocked from the historical memory of the same community.

Contemporary poetry was arriving too, in English and other languages of the community. The lyrics of this protest song were translated from the Bengali:

Trade Union Song of Bangladeshi Workers

We were called from a distant land,
Counting the waves
Of thirteen rivers and seven seas
With hopes of a better life.
We are the workers!
We labour in the factories and the workshops.
If we unite
We can grasp our rights in our hands.
Of course we must unite
If we want to defeat the racist
If we want to break the teeth
Of the bloodsuckers who exploit us.
We must stand together
Under the trade union banner!
Trade Union!
   Trade Union!
     Trade Union!
       TRADE UNION![6]
        Abdus Salique

Many other examples of the literature and curriculum we employed were printed in *The World in a Classroom*, as was the response of the students in the forms of stories, plays, poems and descriptive passages. We made much of the fact that the Victorian brick buildings of our school were constructed during the same time as significant events were happening in the next street. For in Dod Street, yards away from our classroom, the great poet and pioneer socialist, William Morris, led the campaign to establish free speech at open-air political meetings on the corner of that very street where ironically, now a labour exchange stood and the unemployed sought work. We read some of Morris' poems, sang his 'March of the Workers' and wrote a verse and chorus across the high walls of the classroom on huge white sheets. We taught and celebrated the achievements of local history made by local people who had come in their thousands to support Morris and make it impossible for the police to move them on. Like those pioneers we sang:

What is this, the sound and rumour?
What is this that all men hear?
Like the wind in hollow valleys when the storm
 is drawing near,

Like the rolling on of ocean in the eventide of fear?
'Tis the people marching on.

The students were enthusiastic, motivated. They were an internationalist community: in my class of some 30 students we once traced 32 countries of national origin from Guyana to Burma and Hong Kong, from Ireland to St Lucia and Ghana, and projected these proudly on a large map of the world on the classroom wall. Thus they responded to the internationalist history of their own part of London, the arriving place, the 'first anxious halt of the stranger'.[7] History gave them a broad, affirmative narrative theme, but also hundreds of smaller narratives, which they were discovering in the stories they were learning from the curriculum of arrival, interdependence, struggle and progress that was developing in their classrooms. As we read in the lyrics of one of the songs in *Lansbury's Labour Weekly*, 'We mix from many lands, we march from very far'.[8]

There was the Barbadian boy writing about the Bow matchgirls' struggle against the industrial disease 'phossy-jaw', inspired by the lyrics from Bill Owen's musical about the strike:

I've got an onion
With my bread,

I know what
I've got in my bread –
PHOSPHORUS!

Every day we eat it
Every day the same.

We don't have to buy it,
Every bit comes free,
But not long now for me,
I've bought a brand new oak tree.

Goodbye mum, Goodbye dad,
What do you know?
Getting buried tomorrow.

Trevor

There were the stories re-living the schools' strikes in East London in 1911, when the children came out partly in solidarity with their fathers, partly in protest against the authoritarian regimes in their schools:

Our Strike in 1911

My name is Willy Brown, I live in an old house. My Mum died when I was born, and my Dad works in the docks. One day I had to start my new school. So my Dad said, 'you'll be better off at Farrance Street.' I went there and got in. So the next day I tripped to school. In those days I had to go by foot. Everyone looked at me and laughed. I went into school and was put in a class. There were some very bossy boys in there. They asked me questions, so I didn't take no notice, just carried on working all by myself. When it was time to go, I went by the school gates and walked home. When I got in my father asked me if I liked it at school. I said, 'Yes, not bad Dad, why aint you at work?' He said 'I'm on strike because I want more money to feed and look after you better. I can't manage with the money I get.'

I agreed with my father so the next day I told all my friends of my dad going on strike. So one boy said 'your Dad's right. Let's go on strike and stick and stand by our fathers. They do need more money, I think so. My Dad works all through the week, even on weekend days too.' We all went on strike with our Dads, all the school went on strike. We thought it was funny, so we played out.

Then after a few days my Dad got a letter through the post, and it was from the company he works at. They had agreed to give my Dad and the other dockers more money. So my Dad went to work again, and I went to school with all my new friends! Me and my Dad then lived happily together, and we invited some friends to tea. We said we won't get the cane much now, but if we do, I was going to strike again. I told my Dad, and he told me to go on strike again about caning and hitting. He was very pleased with me, and very proud that he had a boy like me!

Theresa

These stories of childhood provoked fascination and the urge to write more and more. Our colleague's General Strike story about the red ties became a favourite. One boy, a skilled and enthusiastic rhymester, wrote a poem based upon the incident, which begins:

> I woke up in the morning
> Everything was bare,
> I went to get my breakfast
> And to comb my scruffy hair.
>
> I looked out of the window
> I could not see a moving thing,
> Not even a big dirty dog
> Clattering on a tin.
>
> I put on my school clothes
> And a red tie,
> It dangles all about
> From my neck down to my flies.

He meets a 'City gent' trying to break the strikers' picket lines and enter the City of London to reach his office:

Then one posh person gets off the coach
'Let us get to work, you striking, filthy dummy!
You pigs may be striking
But we want to earn some money.'

Then a big strong worker
Whose muscles are like steam-rollers,
Stretches the man's hat over his head
And made it five bits of a bowler!

Philip

One of the most engaging topics we covered involved the struggle of the East London Federation of Suffragettes, who campaigned during the years before 1914. The experiences in Holloway Prison of one of their leaders, Sylvia Pankhurst, inspired some moving writing – particularly when the students re-lived her force-feeding, a part of the government's attempt to break her hunger strike. This was Dawn's imagining:

I was arrested on Saturday the 15th of July, and I was put into Holloway Prison. At first I slept in a tiny cell which was very dark and dingy and I only slept for a little while because I was so worried about what was going to happen to me tomorrow.

When morning came, I was taken into a room in which there was a table, a doctor holding a long tube, a large container filled with some hot liquid and three wardresses.

I suddenly realised what was going to happen and struggled hard to get out, but I was overpowered by the wardresses and dragged to the table on which I was laid. I was held down by the wardresses while the doctor forced a long tube up my nose. I screamed, not only with pain, but also fright, for I thought that I would surely die if this pipe went any further. My nose was throbbing and bleeding very fast on the inside. Then the tube went high up to the top of my nose and down on into my throat. I heaved with sickly pain. I thought that I couldn't survive another minute of it. I could hardly breathe and I felt as though I was being strangled from the inside. Then the tube was shoved into my stomach. I was burning all over and my head was throbbing. I tried to vomit it up but it was shoved down still further. Then suddenly my inside burned so much that I half believed that boiling oil was being poured into me. At last the liquid reached my stomach and my whole body shook so much that I thought my bones were going to whizz off and I thought that I would be glad because then there would be an end to this terrible pain. If I was about to die, then the prison would probably be in trouble for letting such a thing happen.

By this time one of the wardresses was crying, and I wondered if she was sorry for me.

As the red hot liquid kept pouring into me, and I kept vomiting it back up, I felt as though I was being tortured to death, for I did not believe for one minute that I would live through this terrible day, and as they dragged me out, I screamed for God to save me from this tremendous pain, and I hoped that I would die before the next feeding time came.

I was left in my filthy cell, in my bloody clothes, just lying there feeling worse than I had ever felt before, in my whole life. I could hear the screaming from the next cell as they dragged Betty Clover into the force-feeding room. I could do nothing at all, I didn't even have the strength to cry.

And Dawn's classmate, Tony, showed that Sylvia Pankhurst's struggle inspired the other gender too:

Force Feeding

> Their feet came stamping on the stone floor,
> Their feet banging like the sounds of war,
> The pipe in my throat ripped and tore,
> They left my cell, I fell to the floor.
> I wish they wouldn't come any more,
> They'll come tomorrow, it's their kind of law,
> I wish they wouldn't come any more.

These children, writing, studying, reflecting, looking around them at their classmates and neighbours, saw more and more that they were creating their poems and stories at the intersection of race and class. Whether they were black or white themselves, they could identify with the makers of their multiracial history and understand the contribution of all peoples. Thus a Pakistani boy could become the voice of George Lansbury, the leader of Poplar Council imprisoned, with his fellow councillors, for refusing to raise the rates: 'We shall again breathe the freshness of freedom like all others. We are not different. After this imprisonment we are again going to fight for our equal rights! Why should we pay for what we have already paid?'

And a white girl could understand in her heart and her head, in cool economic as well as passionate truth, that the life around her was the product of *all* the people who lived in her world:

Our Black Brothers

> Brown, black, white or red
> We must all go to work to earn our own bread,
> Either day in a factory
> Or night in a train
> In a boiling hot sun or a freezing cold rain.
>
> We can't afford to make a fuss
> Who works on our roads or drives a bus,

'cause if we do
They'll all go back
And England will be useless, and that's a fact.

England called, and thank God it did,
'cause they've helped our country to earn a few quid,
In East End and West End
And country too,
The black man's our hero, who made our towns new.

Allison

So what did our constant establishment critics make of all this? Again, even before *The World in a Classroom* was published, with a strong and affirmative introduction by Trevor Huddleston ('It needs great energy, great dedication and great enthusiasm to generate the kind of concern amongst teenagers which will find such positive and creative expression as this book provides'), the education correspondent of *The Times* had, unknowingly to the organizers and myself, surreptitiously joined a teachers' meeting in a pub in Hackney, where I gave a talk about our 'local history' curriculum. Under the unusual (for *The Times*) headline 'Workers Struggles Inspire Pupils' Poems', he gave an account of the meeting, putting particular emphasis on my description of how the London dockers had supported the Russian Revolution by refusing to load an arms ship, the Jolly George, going to the revolution's enemies:

In 1920 local dockers had refused to load arms for use against the Russian Revolution. A pupil had pretended to be a docker and had written a poem about how the benefits of the Russian Revolution were explained to him.
The event was linked by Mr. Searle to the recent refusal by the National Union of Seamen to load ships in Liverpool to carry arms to Chile.
He said: 'There is tremendous material in local history which gives the children not only a basic body of knowledge of the past, but also some kind of incentive to act on in the future. It gives them the knowledge that will be useful in fighting attacks on them now.'

The correspondent then kindly approached my headteacher for his comments, but was perhaps surprised by what he heard. For I was now working in a much more supportive framework:

Mr. P.L.T. Andrews, the school's headmaster told me yesterday: 'I judge the work of Mr. Searle in the classroom. I am quite satisfied with what he is doing. What he may have said at the meeting is his own affair. He is not indoctrinating the children politically.'
Mr. Searle denied that he was using the children for his own ideas. 'I do not think they are empty vessels and you pour facts into them,' he said. 'Unless their minds are there they will not write freely. I encourage them to argue. I want my classes to be fresh and relevant.'[9]

A much more unambiguously hostile article greeted the publication of the book, on the editorial page of the *Daily Telegraph*, under the punny headline 'School that goes for High Marx'.[10] Godfrey Barker's examination of 'Oppression Studies in the East End' (the sub-headline of the same article) tries a sarcastic tack from its first paragraph:

> Mr. Christopher Searle is a thoroughly modern school teacher. He is so greatly concerned with 'racism' that it has become the main subject that he teaches. His classroom, as indeed all classrooms in his school – Langdon Park Comprehensive, Limehouse, East London – is a resistance bunker from which hostility to Mr. Powell, the National Front and 'racism' ebbs forth.

Yet despite the clumsy aggression of the entire article, Barker still acknowledges the skills of the young writers, their 'strong humanitarian feelings', their capacity to 'write very well' despite what they write about. 'They write with innocence and vigour, in optimistic contrast to the gloom of their curriculum,' he declares. In this he is partly right – as Nelson Mandela described his own attitude of mind during his decades in prison, these children's writings also showed the qualities of 'optimism and struggle'.

Education, the weekly magazine of education officers and directors, gave *The World in a Classroom* to a Leeds headteacher to review. He commented that the 'material was aimed at thirteen year-old children: the Jesuits preferred to catch them earlier', and argued that the 'unrelieved diet of oppression from the distorting glass of the left-wing alternative press' is a form of brainwashing. Better, he argued, to deal with fantasy 'if it is needed and brings comfort'.[11] His main assertion however, was that the curriculum we devoloped 'lacks completely the humility of outlook and questioning spirit any good teacher should possess' – an interesting point, considering that the entire basis of the pedagogy was to question the status quo and look at the alternatives that history has rehearsed. But to construct such alternatives with young people, recall and interpret them from the past and work through them as real events in their historical memories – all this, it appears, is a form of tyranny: 'Indeed, in his classroom world, Mr Searle is a dictator, intent on making his charges dance to his tune'.

This headteacher's words were eagerly grasped by Rhodes Boyson MP in a subsequent *Times* article warning of the dangers of 'political education' in schools, in particular that form of it which sets aside 'respect for the monarchy'.[12]

A more unusual set of criticisms came from the libertarian children's author, Leila Berg, a supporter of the 'de-schooling' movement and opponent of compulsory education. Unlike the children of the Tuscan 'free' school of Barbiana, she recognized that 'in Limehouse, London, the kids are forced by law to go to school. They are forced by law – or as good as to go to a *particular* school (in this case, Chris Searle's) and once there, to *his* class. It is not their chosen situation. However friendly he is, however frank in his talk ... his teaching is based, like the teaching of any Tory teacher at a state school, on different levels of coercion ... If the children were free, and could make their own choice about going to school, how would he get his recruits?'[13] Perhaps it is this sense of coercion, she continued, that marks most of the children's writing as 'third-rate and unfelt'.

As a proponent of universal, compulsory state schooling, I could not agree with her central premise. But beyond that, I knew that the motivation and enthusiasm of the students for the local history work was vibrant and strong – and it was clear to me that *that* sense was coming across in their creative writing. The de-schooling arguments had never convinced me, even when I heard them person-to-person during an interview I had with the doyen of the de-schoolers – Ivan Illich, author of *Deschooling Society* – in 1974. He had said to me that the teacher in a compulsory state school could never be more than a 'good prostitute', who gave some occasional bought hours of insight and pleasure to bored and alienated students.[14]

An answer to Leila Berg's points came in a letter to the journal *Books and Bookmen*, which had originally published her review. It was written by a teacher-writer, Marie Peel, who had taken part in some of our teaching sessions that had provoked the students' writing. In a fair and accurate account, she wrote:

> I spent three and a half terms working half a day a week in the school in Poplar where Chris Searle worked, beginning in the hot summer of 1976 when racialism suddenly erupted like an ugly plague. I saw three sessions of the team-teaching underlying the book, enough to recognise a strong framework of information as well as, in this instance, strong propaganda against racism. In the key session Searle led with an account of the many waves of immigration coming to that area over the past 200 years – Irish, Chinese, Jews, West Indian, Cypriot, Indian, Bangladeshi, Ugandan, Asian. Not just who came but why and what work they were usually put to do. By question and quite free response he got corroborative detail from a number of the ninety or so second year students at the session, while by show of hands he quickly established that a large majority had at least one non-London or non-English family connection. One or two of the teachers contributed their own details. (For instance, I mentioned having had a French grandfather, a cabinet maker, who came to East London from Alsace around 1860 because of strong anti-French discrimination after the Franco-Prussian War.)
>
> But the main opportunity for the students to explore and reach some individual understanding of the material came afterwards in their four separate classrooms. In the class I was with, after some lively discussion that was certainly not unduly controlled or directed by the teacher, the students were asked to write about their impressions, real or imagined, or being an immigrant in London. This could be in prose, free verse or play form. I remember an Irish boy's poem, 'I am an Immigrant', that for me suddenly gave compelling new substance to our slang phrase, 'taking the mick'.

> They call me Potato Merchant
> They call me Paddy
> They call me Spud man
> I am proud to be Irish
> I would hate to be English
> They call me what they want
> They are mongrels themselves.

The individual quality of this, and especially the power of the final image, hardly came from indoctrination.

Marie Peel's description – in this case of my colleague Irene Payne's class – was typical of our pattern of working. Each 'theme' or series or events we were considering was begun by a lesson combining the three or sometimes four classes and was largely informational, using various handouts and with contributions and questions from students and teachers. This was followed by a breaking-up into separate classes, and a further separation into small groups of two to four students each. In this context the creative work would develop, in a collaborative and informal classroom ethos. The notion of a dictatorial, Squeers-like or brainwashing ambiance was an enormous distance from the truth of these lessons. The results which emerged in the students' work were, of course, partly based upon the new material that was a foundation for reflection, but it was the application and energy of their creative language in the act of imagining that sparked them into their *own* work, arrived at through their own brain-power and empathy.

This was understood second time around by Geoffrey Summerfield, who reviewed *The World in a Classroom* for the *Times Educational Supplement*. He had not liked *Classrooms of Resistance*, and perhaps the expectation was that he would write a similarly antipathetic review of this new compilation. In fact he set down the opposite, declaring that the 'pupils' writings vindicate his [*our*] programme; they write with verve, wit and compassion, not only as themselves but also through a variety of assumed personae'. Justifying the curriculum that we were striving to develop, he added:

> Given the world as it is, there is no shortage of suitable situations and events. The curriculum is around us, daily. The choice of examples must depend on one's own priorities: one has to choose, even by default. But to carp at *this* selection of topics would be to miss the essential virtues and strengths of the youngsters' writings.
>
> His new book offers a way forward for anyone involved in a multi-ethnic teaching situation; it is full of hope and sublinear energy.[15]

'Hope ... sublinear energy' – both needed for action which arises from knowing and reflecting, a point made strongly by the reviewer for the journal *Christian Action*, when he wrote: 'Above all it is an extraordinarily poetic and moving book. This is poetry not of the ethereal kind, but that which energises one into reflection and action'.[16] And he was right. For the 'ethereal' was never our concern, rather the concrete circumstances and prospects facing our children. How can we help them change what is real? How to mobilize poetry, the imagination and literacy for human betterment? History and its narratives are enacted at the centre of that pedagogy: not the 'subjects' of history but its process as part of the lives of learners and teachers, through what the Guyanese novelist Wilson Harris has called 'the leap of the unfinished genesis of the imagination'.[17]

An understanding of our history – as long as it is *our* history, the history of the ordinary people of this world and all its struggling communities – gives us a secure confidence that just as those who came before could act to make things better, in conditions that were harder, more fraught and challenging, then so can we now. As Harold Rosen wrote, understanding our purpose in the classroom, we were 'concerned with working-class identity, not with how to create an individual awareness so frail that it will melt in the heat of the production line'[18] – *or* the dole queue, *or* the kitchen.

Notes

1 Peter McLaren, *Critical Pedagogy and Predatory Culture*, Routledge, London, 1975.
2 Chris Searle, *The World in a Classroom*, Writers and Readers Cooperative, London, 1977.
3 *The People Marching On*, Langdon Park School, London, 1976.
4 The poems and texts quoted are to be found in *The World in a Classroom* (op. cit.) unless other sources are given.
5 From Chris Searle (ed.), *Bricklight: Poems from the Labour Movement in East London*, Pluto Press, London, 1980.
6 Chris Searle, *Bricklight*, op. cit.
7 Chris Searle, *Bricklight*, op. cit.
8 See introduction to Chris Searle, *Bricklight*, op. cit.
9 *The Times*, 11 March 1976.
10 *Daily Telegraph*, 24 September 1977.
11 *Education*, 2 December 1977.
12 *The Times*, 31 January 1978.
13 Leila Berg, 'Freedom or Indoctrination', *Books and Bookmen*, February 1978.
14 See article by Chris Searle, 'The Good Prostitute', *Radical Education*, Spring 1975.
15 *Times Educational Supplement*, 4 December 1977.
16 *Christian Action*, January 1977.
17 Wilson Harris, *Jonestown*, Faber & Faber, London, 1996.
18 Harold Rosen, 'Out There or Where the Masons Went', *English in Education*, 9 (1), 1975.

7

WINGS OF RACISM

Cover by Dan Jones

I was one of but a handful of white people among tens of thousands black Mozambicans in Nampula football stadium in February 1976, when I heard the president of the new nation, Samora Machel, declare:

Racism, whether it is white in relation to blacks, or blacks in relation to whites, is one of the most degrading and humiliating forms of the system of the exploitation of man by man, the instrument preferred by the reactionary classes to divide, isolate and wipe out the progressive forces.

The complexes which are manifested express the weight of the old mentality which we still carry inside us. The struggle for us to destroy this inheritance is one of the essential moments of creation of the new mentality.[1]

Machel continued to explain how racism had been harnessed and used by the systems of European and American imperialism, directly causing slavery, war, colonialism and the forced subjugation of millions of Africans. 'And yet,' he added 'we do not blame the ordinary people of Portugal, or Britain, or France or America for this. They have often been our friends. It is the system of imperialism that has always been, and still is our enemy'.

For me this was another moment of intense learning, provided for me by Africa – as I was to have hundreds more in the two years that I spent teaching in the Nampula Secondary School, in northern Mozambique. With little knowledge of Portuguese, the national language, I was employed as a teacher of English, and assigned as a personal tutor to a form equivalent to the lower sixth in a British school. Perhaps the students understood my difficulties with Portuguese as many of them were having the same problems, learning it as a second language to Macua, the regional language of most of Nampula province. Certainly they were hugely motivated to learn English – a language, they felt, which would put them into greater communication with much of their own continent and the rest of the world.[2]

During that time, Mozambique was a nation of poets, and they needed little motivation from me to write, and to write in their beginners' English too. José Maria wrote this just a few weeks after putting his mind to the new language:

The Worker Yesterday

Dawn . . .
The worker thinks
thinks of the whip.

Dawn . . .
The worker thinks
thinks of the dust in the mines.

Dawn . . .
The worker thinks
thinks he is capable.

> Dawn . . .
> Now the worker
> thinks of the communal tasks.[3]

These students lived in a country seeking to build a new, antiracist society after centuries of racist, colonial rule, yet were being hemmed in by a racist regime in the west – Rhodesia, which was constantly violating their territory and killing their people, and the apartheid government of South Africa on their southern frontiers. They wrote poems of solidarity with the people of Zimbabwe (as Rhodesia would one day again become) or anywhere in the world where people were struggling for a just society:

> I'll fight with you, brother
> in Zimbabwe,
> to destroy British colonialism,
>
> We'll fight together
> for we're boughs of the same tree,
> to share the same sap
> sons of Mother Africa.

Americo Cassimo

Or, as in 'Blood in Five Continents':

> Our freedom isn't complete
> While there are oppressed people,
> Our life will be incomplete
> While workers continue subjugated.
>
> In Chile and Namibia
> In imperialism's cage
> Blood irrigates the prisons –
> In bantustans of South Africa
> in suburbs of tin in Portugal
> the children die of hunger.

Antonio Cateu

They proudly and ambitiously saw their own country and its revolution as an example which would travel across Africa, and then through the world of oppressed peoples:

> Africa
> Exploited and oppressed
> Today rises and says,
> 'Freedom, workers of the world.'

Antonio Cateu

These students knew viscerally from their own very recent history the way the system of imperialism works. Joaquim tried to express it as an ordinary Mozambican before the end of Portuguese colonial rule might:

> I arise
> I look through the window of my bedroom
> And I say
> It's time . . .
> The clearness of the growing day
> is the end of my joy!
> Because I know to whom the day belongs,
> More than a drop of my blood
> will be sucked,
> because I know who profits from my work –
> and my money, paid in taxes
> will be used to buy more guns
> more grenades
> to assassinate my people
> to oppress my people,
> to hold me back when I say I'm exploited,
> to force me to pay more taxes
> ahhhhh . . .
> I'm a peasant
> from the rising to the setting of the sun
> in the black dust of the exploited earth.
> I'm a worker
> I'm a fighter for freedom
> I'm a poor worker.

These students, like all students in Mozambican schools at the time, worked collaboratively in groups deliberately developed to bring together the more advanced and less advanced, and in an intensely democratic framework which encouraged cooperation, confidence and creative innovation. They read out their work to each other in an open and trusting atmosphere that made positive virtues out of criticism and self-criticism and within which individual insights were shared and developed. The school had various stages and fora for the democratic participation of students and teachers – something I began to understand immediately, when on my first day at school, I walked in while the teachers were electing the commission that would lead the school as a replacement for the colonial headteacher. All these developments were almost like a wish-fulfilment for me, who along with thousands of other British teachers in our school and trade unions, had been struggling for something similar in our own contexts for many years. It seemed that the democratic and creative approaches to learning English which motivated these students, and to which they responded with such enthusiasm and learning attainment, should also be working in English classrooms – particularly as they were based on an understanding and rejection of the old colonial-fascist ethos in their country's schools that went before, and a thirst for discovery and invention in teaching and learning based upon the real world around them, its concrete problems and underdeveloped resources.

When I returned to East London in 1979 I carried back everything that I had learned in Africa with me. Almost as soon as I had arrived, I found myself swept into the mounting anger and protest in Hackney and Stepney at the increased levels of racism on the streets, the continuing menace of fascist groupings like the National Front and the British Movement, and the hostile attitude of the police towards black youth – and their reluctance to check the growth of street racism following the racist murders of the Asian young men, Altab Ali and Kennith Singh.

There was one particularly horrific incident that had broken out on the streets of the East London district of Stoke Newington in December 1978, that dominated the anger of this protest movement. In the late evening of December 10, a black 19-year-old, Michael Ferreira, and a group of his friends, were returning home from a disco when they were provoked and attacked by a group of white youths, who hurled racist insults at them and then attacked them, resulting in a serious knife injury to Michael. Unable to find an unvandalized phone box, Michael's friends half-carried him into Stoke Newington police station and asked the officers on duty whether they could use the telephone to call an ambulance. The policemen prevaricated while Michael bled heavily, asking provocative questions and suggesting that it was he and his friends who had caused the trouble. Eventually the ambulance was called, and Michael died on the way to the hospital.

It was a grotesque example of a deadly racist attack with the added dimension of police connivance and inaction, and it preceded a further black death in the same police station, when ex-Sir John Cass school student Colin Roach died from shotgun wounds to the head after he was arrested and detained there in January 1983. The Michael Ferreira tragedy provoked strong indigation among the multiracial group of 14-year-olds that I found myself teaching in January 1979, having returned to Langdon Park School immediately upon coming home to East London from Mozambique two weeks before. Despite the different realities of a revolutionary school in northern Mozambique and a state comprehensive in East London, the students had many similar qualities of creative energy and an acute consciousness about injustice and racism in the world so close around them. So it did not seem strange at all to reorganize the class using the same group structures that were integral to the school system in Mozambique, and develop a process of literacy teaching that used that real world around them and its authentic words and dialogue as the source of learning and teaching – including the central creative processes of poetry and playwriting.

The writing of plays presents rich and engaging scope for the process of critical literacy. Essentially a collaborative classroom activity, there is always an opportunity for continuous dialogue and cooperative insight, experimentation, and a wide variety of roles and functions for the participants, as well as the framework for a genuinely democratic working method. Using the 'Mozambican' method of splitting the class into four working groups, each group based around a judicious student mix of ability, gender, culture and level of confidence, I encouraged the students to read newspaper accounts of the death of Michael Ferreira and the protests that had been provoked as a result of it, and the reaction of his family and friends. As expected, some of the students already knew about the events, particularly those from Caribbean families. Others immediately had other grim incidents to relate about their brothers' or cousins' encounters with the police in East London. I suggested the idea of a collective play, and this was greeted enthusiastically. I said that we needed an introductory poem that gave an overall sense of the writers' attitudes towards the play's incidents, and a Jamaican girl and Mauritian boy were assigned to that task by a group of their classmates: 'They're good writers!' was the general judgement. Soon the pair had come up with these few lines which were read out to the rest of the class, and seemed to establish an agreement from everyone involved. This would set the mood and atmosphere for what was to follow:

> The evil wings of racism have once again
> spread over this country,
> The evil that has brought fear –
> and I warn my black brothers
> if they see or hear racism –
> stay clear![4]

The 'preface' ended with this strong couplet, setting down the function of the play-to-be-written:

> Get together, let the people know,
> there'll be no fun if the Nazis grow!

Each of the four groups was given a particular part of the narrative to dramatize: the attack on the street, the scene in the police station, the reaction of the boys' families, the protests following the authorities' refusal to release Michael's body to the family. Each group offered a reading of the scene that they had written to the rest of the class, and suggestions and amendments were offered and made to the 'text'. What resulted was a composite creative endeavour which was certainly unified in its tone of indignation and protest, and, in its own plain and unambiguous way, offered a dramatic narrative of the horrific events. 'Agit-prop' theatre it was, but it offered more. As the boys come home from the disco, their dialogue is steeped in sexist banter – there is no attempt to idealize them as characters or sanitize their speech. Suddenly, as if out of nowhere, they are attacked and one of them is stabbed, and they look around for a way of calling for help. They realize they might as well be miles away from any resources for their injured friend: there is only the enemy close at hand. The starkness of the dialogue suddenly reveals the truth of their predicament:

TONY: What's going on?

DELROY: Hey, what happened to Michael?

GEORGE: One of them bloody skinheads knifed him.

TONY: Don't muck about now, what happened?

GEORGE: They stabbed him, I tell you!

DEXTON: Don't stand there chatting – look he could be bleeding to death.

TONY: Where's the nearest call box? He needs an ambulance.

DELROY: It's just round the corner.

TONY: Let's go then.

> [*Tony and Delroy run off.*]

DEXTON [*supporting Michael*]: It's all right Michael, we're going to get the ambulance for you.

GEORGE: Yeh, it'll be here in no time.

MICHAEL: Ah-h-h-h-h . . . it really hurts now.

> [*Tony and Delroy run back, breathless.*]

TONY: The bloody thing was broke.

DELROY: Some vandals smashed the phone in.

DEXTON: That's all we need, isn't it?

> [*Michael groans, almost continuously.*]

GEORGE: What are we going to do then? He's really hurt.

LEROY: The nearest phone's in the police station.

GEORGE: What, take him to the Babylon shop? Once we're in there we'll never get out.

LEROY: What choice have we got – look how he's bleeding.

GEORGE: All right then, let's get him down there.

MICHAEL [*almost delirious*]: Yeh . . . come on . . . take me there.

DEXTON: Oh Christ, I suppose we'll have to.

LEROY: Bloody Hell, I hope it's all right.

Language could not be more naked than this. There is nothing 'extra' here, nothing gratuitous or unnecessary. Words are simple, falling into their places without affectation – as they frequently do, inadequately but concretely so, in real life. That same bareness characterized the scene inside Stoke Newington Police station during the late hours of an East-End Saturday night, as the boys met the wall of the law:

POLICEMAN 1: What do you lot want?

POLICEMAN 2: What have you been up to?

POLICEMAN 1: Yeh – what's going on?

GEORGE: Please . . . look, our friend's bleeding. Can we call an ambulance?

POLICEMAN 1: Hold your horses. I want to know exactly what's going on here.

GEORGE: There aint time for that – look how he's bleeding.

POLICEMAN 1: Shut up. Now first of all give us your names and addresses.

GEORGE: Look, just phone for an ambulance first, we'll tell you all about it afterwards.

DEXTON: Yeh, he's hurt you know.

MICHAEL: Please ... help me ... phone for an ambulance.

POLICEMAN 1: Keep quiet son, we'll attend to you in a minute. I've got to take a statement first.

DEXTON: Look – I can tell you very quickly in a few simple words. We were jumped on by three white kids. One of them stabbed him.

POLICEMAN 1: Where was this?

DEXTON: Opposite the park.

POLICEMAN 1: Did you recognise any of them?

DEXTON: No, but we've seen them all down Chapel Street handing out National Front leaflets. Now come on, please call an ambulance.

MICHAEL [*groaning*]: Please ...

> [*Enter a third POLICEMAN.*]

POLICEMAN 3: What's going on here?

POLICEMAN 2: These boys have been starting trouble.

DEXTON: What? We didn't do nothing, they set on us. Now are you going to phone for a bloody ambulance?

POLICEMAN 3: Watch your language with me Sonny. Now, have you lot been in any trouble before?

DEXTON: We were picked up once on SUS.

POLICMAN 3: Ahh! So you started a fight eh? Picked on some white boys eh? Then you got the worst of it and come here with your lies about other kids?

GEORGE [*pushing forward*]: Look, can't you see how our friend is bleeding? Send for an ambulance.

And it continues – the anger and frustration building up to bursting point while Michael bleeds on.

The scenes were put together and the same two students were given the task of writing a final 'chorus' to end the play. Their last four lines were like a mobilizing shout:

> After this, there's no turning back.
> Black and White unite!
> And together we will fight!
> To stop these rats from roaming the streets.

We acted out the play in the classroom, and as the campaign grew in East London to publicize and protest against the circumstances of Michael Ferreira's death, we decided to use the play in whatever way we could to make a contribution. I had already met Michael's mother and told her about the project, and she too thought it would be a useful idea to publish the short play as a pamphlet for young people. I interviewed her and learned some information about her son – his Guyanese childhood, his interest in mechanics and ambition to eventually own his own garage, and this became the basis of a short introduction. The play was published as a pamphlet in support of the campaign under the title *Who Killed Michael Ferreira?* and became a useful vehicle for informing people, in a narrative and dramatic form, about what happened to Michael and his friends.

This again was a 'community' production, intended for use in specific local circumstances, but strangely, the short play became the centre of controversy some nine years later, when it was published as part of an essay on 'English' teaching in a book I wrote called *All Our Words*. This book was part of a series called 'Young World Books' published by the anti-racist organization 'Liberation', which Neil Kinnock, then leader of the Labour Party opposition, had recommended with some complimentary remarks. A right-wing 'parents front' organization called 'Families for Defence'[5] and its sibling group 'Schoolwatch', identified the publications of 'Young World Books' as 'an absolute disgrace ... undermining every aspect of authority', and condemned Kinnock for his support.[6] These were the words of Lady Olga Maitland, 'Schoolwatch's' 'coordinator' and she pointed directly at the play *Who Killed Michael Ferreira?*, which was cited in the House of Commons as a 'thoroughly unpleasant example' of subversive children's classroom work by John Bowis, Conservative MP for Battersea.[7] Typically, Tory newspapers joined in the harangue, neglecting the fact that the play was about a racist murder, and merely stressing that it was about a 'gang of black youths' and that it was 'anti-police' (*Evening Standard*)[8] and 'anti-cop' (the *Sun*)[9]. According to a report in the *Daily Telegraph*,[10] Lady Maitland had persuaded the Department of Education to ask the schools' inspectorate to investigate the play and the other 'Young World Books': 'We are investigating the suitability of these books to be used with children'. She added that schools' minister Angela Rumbold 'shares my concern and has asked to see the books', and an Education Department spokesman confirmed 'Her Majesty's inspectorate are looking at the books in question to see whether or not they are in breach of the law in terms of indoctrination and should be withdrawn'.[11] The spectre of censorship was appearing – this time not invoked by a group of governors in an archaically-constituted East End school, but at the level of the state itself, which was already dealing with other books 'named' for censorship: *Nuclear Weapons and Warfare, The Great War, Russia, 1900–1953* and *How Racism Came to Britain*.[12]

As for the students who collectively wrote *Who Killed Michael Ferreira?* in their East London classroom, by this time they were all well into their twenties. I wondered if they had read these reports about what they had achieved at school all those years before, and remembered the words of a Bangladeshi girl, Tabassum, one of their classmates, who had written and read out loud this poem to them:

> One day
> a tree will grow high and strong
> in the garden of justice
>
> And live forever.[13]

Notes

1 See Chris Searle, *Beyond the Skin*, Liberation Books, London, 1989.
2 Chris Searle, *We're Building the New School!*, Zed Press, London, 1980.
3 This, and other poems by Mozambican students, from Chris Searle, *Beyond the Skin*, op. cit.
4 'Who Killed Michael Ferreira?', in Chris Searle, *All Our Words*, Young World Books, London, 1986.
5 See press release from 'Families for Defence', 26 March 1986.
6 *Daily Mail*, 26 March 1986.
7 *Daily Telegraph*, 29 March 1986.
8 *Evening Standard*, 23 March 1986.
9 The *Sun*, 25 March 1986.
10 *Daily Telegraph*, 29 March 1986.
11 *Morning Star*, 29 March 1986, and *Daily Telegraph*, op. cit.
12 *Tribune*, 15 April 1986, and *Morning Star*, 7 May 1986.
13 Chris Searle (ed.) *Our City: A Collection of Poems by London School Students*, Young World Books, London, 1984.

BUTTERFLIES OF EL SALVADOR

Poem and illustration by Sean, 13

In June 1983 at a talk at the London University Institute of Education, I committed what apparently was an unforgiveable crime by arguing the case for a critical pedagogy that educated school students about imperialism as well as racism. Perhaps the guardians of British culture felt vulnerable defending a system that had been their nation's greatest crime in history – a crime which was now the leading foreign policy priority of Britain's closest and most powerful ally, the United States of America.

My talk, which was later published in the progressive teachers' journal, *Teaching London Kids*,[1] began in this way:

I want to talk about education for resistance, and in particular ask the question: why teach the struggle of the people in El Salvador, or Chile, or Argentina, or Uruguay, or Guatemala, to the children in our London classrooms? For we are asking this question in the light of our own union, the National Union of Teachers, formally taking the important decision to support the struggle of ANDES, the teachers' union in El Salvador, that is a part of the liberation movement there.

When we come to consider multicultural education, we know it is all things to all people. Anti-racist education is now much defended by teachers throughout the country, but it has taken a long struggle to reach the point where the ILEA [Inner London Education Authority] is making it compulsory policy for all their schools. They will have to formulate their policy with the participatory and democratic energy of London's teachers and they will have to live up to it and resource it seriously. But the third stage, anti-imperialist education, is something which challenges everything in our society and in the wider world that is oppressive.

For as soon as we begin to teach about conditions and struggles in such countries as El Salvador, we are beginning to help our children understand the role of imperialism in the world; the role of multinational interests, international financial and economic intrigue and an oppression which exploits, works through yet is beyond racism – which is only one of its strategies. And as we enter into that kind of struggle with knowledge and consciousness, we are indisputably talking about the source of imperialism in the world, the United States of America.

All this may seem a million miles away from where I was teaching at the time, in a boys' comprehensive school in Bethnal Green, East London. But I had just returned from working for two years in the teacher education programme of Grenada, in the Caribbean, within what was effectively the first English-speaking revolutionary process in modern history, and had felt the full impact of the many dimensions of US aggression – political, economic, journalistic, military and trade destabilization, all of which was to prove but a prelude to the eventual invasion of the island in October 1983.[2]

I was also more and more conscious that the students whom I was teaching in East London were studying in our classrooms and living in the neighbouring streets – their fathers at work in the small clothing factories in and around Brick Lane and Spitalfields, their mothers at home struggling in a new land with little or no English and the constant threat of racism on the streets outside their front doors – all precisely *because* of imperialism. The questions sprang from the classroom itself. Why was the Greek Cypriot boy there, sitting next to his friend from St Vincent? What about the boy from Hong Kong in the corner, or the Jamaican boy, so full of questions, joking with the boy from Turkey? How did that Sikh boy come to be here? What had happened in the life of the family of that boy from Nigeria to bring him here, to an East London school? As the Bradford textile worker answered the question 'Why are you over here?', put to him by a white journalist: 'We are here because you were there'. An understanding of the root causes of imperialism and its new potency under changed political and economic forces was an entirely legitimate area of engagement for critical literacy and imaginative writing – the context cried out for it. I also very soon discovered that it was a subject which very keenly motivated the 13- and 14-year-old boys whom I was teaching, and it sparked their reading and writing interest for a period of several weeks.

I decided to concentrate upon the context of Latin America because it was in that region of the world that the US response to internal events within nominally independent nations had been at its most interventionist and venomous. The open US support for the 1973 military coup in Chile, the continuous attempts to undermine and destroy the Sandinista Revolution in Nicaragua, the daily aid given to the brutal forces suppressing the popular rebellion of the people of El Salvador – there was a whole curriculum of modern imperialism here, and much to study and reflect upon also in the courage of those resisting it, and the literature that they were creating in the process.

The first task was to locate and bring together some of this literature, and appraise its suitability for 13- and 14-year-olds. I used some of the narrative poems of Pablo Neruda, in particular 'Jose Cruz Achachalla',[3] which tells with graphic realism of the life and work of a Bolivian tin miner crippled with silicosis. There was a pressing reason for introducing this poem at this time. It was during the months of the British miners' strike (1983–4) and the teachers at the school had developed a solidarity link with Shirebrook, a mining village in North Derbyshire. Two striking mineworkers were visiting the school and talking to the students during that particular week, so Neruda's words and images were given even more meaning and power as the students shared the lives of miners from Bolivia and Britain. A boy from a Greek Cypriot family used his imaginative empathy and simple, naked words to write this:

Copper Miners in Chile

I work in the copper mine
I work in all the dust.
I work from morning to night,
I don't know when morning or night is
Because it is so dark.

I suffer a lot
I suffer from silicosis from the dust.
We risk our lives for rich men
Who sit behind desks drinking coffee
That our wives picked,
And eat our corn and our wheat.
I got kicked out of my job yesterday
Because of my silicosis.
I went home to my children who are illiterate.
They asked me, 'why are you home, father?'
I said, 'to see you, my children.'
But they knew that there was something
On my mind that I cannot shake off.
Last week there was a gas explosion,
My best mate died.
I had to go to his house
To tell his wife and three children.
He would have died anyway,
He had silicosis, like me.
Oh yes, I will die soon,
But before I die
I want to see my family
For the last few days of my life.

Michael

Mark, who sat next to Michael, seemed to combine the experience and narrative of the two continents of mineworkers:

Sweating all day long
Sweating all night long,
When I approach daylight
My eyes just blur.
I'm dying now,
I'm washing away my life.

The pursuit of relevant texts was made easier when the school's English department bought a set of the young people's novel *Talking in Whispers*,[4] by James Watson. This is set in Chile during the coup and its aftermath. Written by an Englishman, it succeeds dramatically in re-living the effect of fascist violence on a teenage boy and his family, and concentrates on describing the activities of the Chilean junta's secret police, the CNI. The novel provoked a number of imaginative and insightful stories among the students. This one, 'Maria's Story', was written by Aroz, a Bangladeshi boy:

I was at my uncle's house. It was about a mile away from my house, down a narrow, hilly road. My Dad worked in a hospital for the poor and they were going to protest about the government. That night, when I was sleeping at my uncle's house I thought I heard a jeep go past on the road. Then I said to myself that it was nothing and I went back to sleep.

Next morning I woke up, got dressed and ate my breakfast. Then I said that I was going home. I was skipping along the dusty road feeling happy. When I got to my village I was amazed to see that my house was not there. I went near the burnt ashes. I saw bits of our furniture, I was in tears, crying because I knew who did it. It was the C.N.I. Then I heard a creak. A door opened. It was our neighbour, an old man who had had his family taken by the C.N.I. He came close to me and put his hand on my shoulder. He told me how they took my Dad, my brother and even my mother. He told me how they dragged them and kicked them to the jeep and then lit a fire. After he told me all that the rain began to fall.

The old man said, 'come to my house and have a cup of coffee,' so I went in. He made me a cup and I drank it. Then I heard a knock on the door. I opened it, it was a man from our village. The old man introduced him and told me that he was the organiser of our protest. He sat down.

'We have got two hundred people so far,' he said.

Another thought came into my head. I said to myself, 'if I go to the protest I'll show the C.N.I. how much I love my Mum and Dad.'

So I said to the man, 'can I join the protest?'

'Tomorrow at the torture house, then we shall march on to the President's palace.' It was getting dark by then, so I went to bed. The old man put a blanket over me and said, 'sleep well.'

Next morning I woke up earlier than usual, got my clothes and ate my breakfast. Then I made my way towards the torture centre. When I got there I saw lots of people standing around, shouting 'C.N.I. out!' I joined in the shouting and was suddenly grabbed by a secret policeman. He punched me so hard that I didn't know where I was. Then he dragged me to a jeep and drove me away quick. I was shouting out to let me go, so one of the men slapped me.

After a while the jeep stopped near a football stadium. I was dragged through the stadium tunnel and kicked into a little room without any light. The room was dark and cold. I could hear people screaming and crying from the torture that the C.N.I. was giving them. Suddenly something moved. It came from the corner of the room but I could not see it because it was too dark. I went near to the corner. I fell over something and screamed. It was a body, all carved up. It had big, nasty bruises on its face. Then I saw it had no eyes nor ears, and I saw a necklace around its neck. It was my father's. Then I saw another body, a woman's body. She had her hair burned and she was naked, with big bruises. It was my mother.

I cried more. Then I saw a hand. It moved. It was a young man. I knew he was my brother. He could not speak but he was trying to say something. He knew me, his eyes told me that. Then the hand suddenly dropped and he did not move. I knew he had died.

Now I was wondering what they were going to do with me. They had killed my father, my mother and even my brother. Twelve hours passed, it was getting even darker and I was shivering by then. I was hungry, but nobody gave me any food. I was getting tired. I tried to sleep but someone came and slapped me and then kicked me and slammed the door. This went on all night, I couldn't sleep because people kept coming in to boot me or punch me or shout into my ear.

When the sun shone, a little bit of light came slowly into a hole in the damp room. Then I heard a creak and I knew that the door had opened again. Someone came in and dragged me out onto a bench and fixed some wires onto my body. Then someone else pressed something onto me and gave me an electric shock. It hurt me so much that I began to scream.

'Who was the leader of the protest?'

'I don't know.'

'Yes you do!'

'Ahhhh, I don't know, really.'

After an hour I couldn't take it any more so I said it was Roberto. 'So at last you've told us!' The other man took the wires off. Then he got four whips and the four men whipped me, kicked me and tortured me until I was half-unconscious. Then a man came in and dragged me out to a truck, full of other half-dead people with some dead already. It went about two miles away from the stadium and dumped us fifty yards away from the road. I managed to crawl along back to the road and I heard a motor cycle. It came nearer and nearer and then it stopped.

The next thing I knew I was in a house sleeping. I saw it was the old man's house. As I slowly got up, the old man came in and said, 'you go to sleep, it will be all right.'

That was three years ago. Still I am affected by the horror that the C.N.I. did to me.

Aroz has stepped squarely into the brutality of the twentieth century to write his story. His language unconsciously borrows from Auschwitz, from Soweto, from Alabama as well as from Santiago. It reflects the brutal repression of his own land of origin under the Pakistani military dictatorship and his people's struggle for national independence just over a decade before. It is the historical memory of his generation, coming from an empathy with all those who have suffered – and his words carry that history.

After considering Chile, the situation in El Salvador became more clear, particularly when we used a section of Manlio Argueta's powerfully moving Salvadorian novel *One Day of Life*[5] as the main text to stimulate the students' own writing. Life for an uneducated recruit in a brutal fascist army was also a theme we pursued, using the story 'Private Eloi'[6] by the Cuban writer Samuel Feijoo, as well as the poem about the soldier who killed Ernesto 'Che' Guevara – Nicolas Guillen's 'Guitar in Mourning Major'[7] and some of the lyrics of the Chilean singer executed by the junta, Victor Jara.[8] This was at least an introduction, albeit a very brief and selective one, to some of the outstanding wordmakers of Latin America. Their projection of real events and surroundings in simple, immediate language had a sharp and poignant effect on the consciousness and writing of many of the students.

One boy, fresh from reading a chapter of *One Day of Life* which told of the effect upon rural Salvadorian families of the death squads of the far-right ARENA (Nationalist Republican Alliance), wrote of the fear and threat which pressed in from all sides:

> One night someone dies
> The next night someone dies –
> When will it be me?
> I hope it won't be me
> As I wake in the morning
> Scared to go downstairs,
> Someone might be down there
> Waiting to kill me.
> Every night I lie awake
> And hope that it's not our house tonight,
> Guns fire, someone's dead,
> Then you hear the jeep pull off.
> Every night
> Every night someone dies
> Every night the jeep comes.
> The shots come from next door,
> Maybe tomorrow it will be me.
> I hope. That's all I can do.
>
> *Dean*

Years later, when I met and interviewed Argueta, I told him about the impact of his book upon the understanding of these 13-year-old East London boys, and how their own solid, picked-out and accurate words had sought to emulate his own. He said that was how he wanted to write, so that ordinary people all over the world – including children – could understand upon their senses the struggle of his people against a brutal government that had behind it the full economic and military resources of the United States of America. I showed him this short poem, part terrifyingly concrete, part almost mystical, by a Jamaican boy, inspired by Argueta's own stark and beautiful language. It had been written across a coloured drawing of a kneeling boy, his eyes transfixed by a giant butterfly:

My Son

> I open my arms like a butterfly
> Trying to keep my son in.
> He's suffering from gastro-enteritis,
> A common disease.
> He doesn't know what to do,
> I am afraid
> He might die
> And leave me alone.

He will go to the heavens
And roam the wilderness,
And come back in reincarnation
Of a butterfly
To bring freedom
To El Salvador.

Sean

For provoking such writing in the classroom and arguing for and defending its content, I found myself at the centre of fresh controversies. 'Beware
these Classroom Ayatollahs!' screamed a headline in the *Daily Express*[9] – meaning teachers such as myself and those advocating peace studies in schools. In
the House of Commons, the Conservative member for Gainsborough and
Horncastle in rural Lincolnshire and co-founder of the pro-NATO pressure
group 'The Coalition for Peace through Security', Edward Leigh MP, quoted
from my speech at the Institute of Education,[10] and as the *Daily Telegraph*
reported, contrived to use 'Mr Searle's prescription for an anti-imperialist
syllabus to lend weight to their campaign for an anti-indoctrination clause
in the Education Act'.[11] He also added that 'the case is instructive in that it
came to light only because the teacher concerned felt confident enough to
advertise his misbehaviour in the radical educational press'.[12] One must not,
it seems, become involved in an open and honest argument, whatever one
does, particularly when the subject is imperialism and the issue is education.
That other scourge of peace studies and curriculum 'reform,' Baroness Cox,
also registered a virtually apoplectic disapproval on the editorial page of the
Daily Mail,[13] under the headline 'Militants who are Getting at your Children'
and beside an ingenious drawing of an assembly of schoolchildren in a playground, shaped as a hammer and sickle.

All this and more letters and exchanges in the *Times Educational Supplement*,[14]
was becoming too much for the Labour-controlled ILEA, who officially
'warned' me by instructing my bemused acting headteacher to hand me a
copy of their curriculum document *History and Social Sciences at Secondary
Level*,[15] and refer me to page 46 and the section about 'teaching controversial
issues in the classroom'. This 'disciplinary' act was widely reported in the
Conservative press. 'Balanced View Warning to Anti-U.S. Teacher', headlined
the *Daily Telegraph*,[16] and even found its way to apartheid South Africa, where
the *Rand Daily Mail* reported the story, again using the expression, 'anti-U.S.
teacher'.[17]

I could only view the affair as an uncanny set of circumstances. Here was
a nation – my own birthplace, whose greatest power arose from its stolen
imperial wealth and which, after the last world war, had exhaustedly passed
over its imperial mantle to the huge and powerful nation that had once been
one of its possessions. Yet that old nation's educational establishment wanted
no open or critical pedagogy upon the subject, particularly when it took as
its starting point those very people most involved, their lives most crushed
and despoiled by this new imperialism. The liberal shell was cracking – in
Bethnal Green too. Perhaps it was too much to hope for support from the

authorities that controlled the school system, and for them to, as one young poet put it, 'open their eyes like an orange that's been peeled' to the system that was trampling so many lives in El Salvador and throughout the world. But as in so many other contexts and circumstances, I felt that my students understood so much more than the adults who presumed to organize and control their education, expressing their wish in the simplest yet most radical and challenging of conceptions:

My Wish

I wish for peace
No more war
My wish

Steak and chips for all
No more hunger
My wish

A warm bed for all children
No more cold
My wish

A friend for everyone
No more loneliness
My wish

People looking after each other
No more fear
My wish for the world

Robert[18]

Notes

1 See 'Links of Resistance', *Teaching London Kids*, 21, Spring 1983.
2 Chris Searle, *Grenada: The Struggle Against Destabilization*, Writers and Readers Cooperative, London, 1983.
3 Chris Searle (ed.), *One for Blair*, Young World Books, London, 1989.
4 James Watson, *Talking in Whispers*, Gollancz, London, 1983.
5 Manlio Argueta, *One Day of Life*, Chatto & Windus, London, 1983.
6 From *Cuba: An Anthology for Young People*, Young World Books, London, 1983.
7 See Chris Searle (ed.), *One for Blair*, op. cit.
8 Joan Jara (ed.), *Victor Jara: His Life and Songs*, Elm Tree Books, London, 1976.
9 *Daily Express*, 9 March 1984.
10 *Hansard*, House of Commons, 31 July 1984.
11 *Daily Telegraph*, 16 January 1984.
12 Quoted from *The Guardian* in *Teaching London Kids*, 22, Spring 1984.
13 *Daily Mail*, 22 April 1985.

14 *Times Educational Supplement,* 25 December 1983 and 6 January 1984.
15 Inner London Education Authority, *History and Social Sciences at Secondary Level,* London, 1983.
16 *Daily Telegraph,* 16 January 1984.
17 *Rand Daily Mail,* Johannesburg, 18 January 1984.
18 From Chris Searle (ed.): *Our City: A Collection of Poems by London School Students,* Young World Books, London, 1984.

9

REMEMBER HILLSBOROUGH

Words of grief and tribute

For Heather Rooney, a YTS trainee in the City Council's Occupational Health unit, poetry proved a way of helping her come to terms with the nightmare of the Hillsborough disaster.

A year ago Heather was a pupil at Herries School in Shirecliffe and had a regular Saturday job at Hillsborough, working in an office against the background of the cheers and roars of the crowd.

She was doing just that when the disaster happened and the poem she wrote afterwards describes graphically how the cheers turned to something else as the scale of the disaster became clear.

Heather's poem is one of a collection of poems by the people of Sheffield, Liverpool and Nottingham – as well as further afield – which have been gathered together by Chris Searle, one of the city's education advisers as a tribute to those who died.

And she read her poem at a special launch of the collection in the Mandela Room nearly one year after the tragedy. Guests included the families of

Heather Rooney reads her poem.

those who died, contributors and Sheffield Wednesday players.

Chris told the guests: "Poetry has always been the way in which ordinary people have expressed themselves when faced with a tragedy of this sort.

"The poems about Hillsborough are not the kind you will find in literary selections but they are the authentic voice of a community coming to terms with a moment of grief.

"And it is to the young people, in particular, that we must listen as so many of those who died were young people with so much beauty inside them."

Copies of 'Remember Hillsborough' can be obtained from the Waterthorpe and Central Library shops and local bookshops.

Courtesy of The Press Office, Sheffield Town Hall

On the afternoon of 15 April 1989, Heather Rooney, a school student who had a Saturday job at the Hillsborough football ground, the home of Sheffield Wednesday Football Club, was working as usual in the office overlooking the playing area as the FA Cup semi-final started between Liverpool and Nottingham Forest.[1] The huge crowd roared as the game began, but something else was happening at the Leppings Lane end of the ground where Liverpool supporters were massed. The scale of the tragedy at Hillsborough that afternoon was awesome. Ninety-six people were to die as a result, suffocated and crushed against the iron fences surrounding the pitch. Later – like thousands of others, some who were there, and many who were not – Heather wrote down her experience in the form of a ballad:

Thoughts of Hillsborough

Sitting in the office,
You could hear the crowd's great roar,
The sun was shining happiness,
So who could ask for more?

The game was just beginning,
When the roaring came to a stop,
No yelling from the stand,
And no singing from the Kop.

It was when I heard the sirens,
That my heart began to pound,
Without a clue what was happening,
To this safe and friendly ground.

I then saw with my eyes this horrid scene,
To see what I could do,
Body to body lay there cold,
Face to face, each blue.

I gave the injured water,
And shared with them their fear,
And for every drop of water,
There also dropped a tear.

The crying from the families,
As they watched their loved ones go,
The tangled scarves and souvenirs,
The fence was crushed down low.

The bells are chiming in the church,
No less than ninety-five,
Ninety-five candles burning constantly,
Representing every lost life.

It breaks my heart to think of it
And remember the fateful sound,
I see her stand there mournfully,
This hurt, but friendly ground.

Heather's brave poem was not intended as a work of art. More a work of
love, a work of memory, a signpost of a terrifying event and a marker that it
must never happen again. For in the days and weeks following the disaster,
hundreds of poems arrived at the Sheffield Education Department, where I
was working at the time – in particular after a Liverpudlian colleague, Steve
Chew, and myself had invited contributions to a memorial anthology that we
were planning to compile. In Liverpool, another anthology, *Words of Tribute*,
was published by the Liverpool University Community Resource Unit – in
collaboration with Liverpool libraries. A special archive was established in
Liverpool Central Library to hold all these poems.

Poems arrived on formal bereavement cards, on postcards, on sheets from
school exercise books and between lines of a letter on airmail paper, as well
as perfectly typeset or elegantly written in a scrupulous longhand. Some were
written, briefly and poignantly, on mere scraps of paper, such as 'Hillsborough
Heartache' by a Mrs Swift of Sheffield, which was among the first to arrive:

Hillsborough Heartache

Yes I cried for fans who died,
And those who are left behind,
Mums and Dads, Lasses and Lads,
You are all on my mind.

Bright was the day,
Happy and gay, were
The fans going to the semi.
Little did we know
On that fateful day,
God would take so many.

They were, in the main, crafted tributes of grief and a terrible sadness.
Poetry was the vehicle for a mass expression of mourning. For the popular
imagination it was the way ordinary people turned when an event was too
hugely tragic for them to contemplate and express through any other means.
On the front cover of the anthology that we eventually published, called
simply *Remember Hillsborough*, there was a photograph of a small bunch of
white flowers that had been tied by a ribbon to the Hillsborough gates.
Attached was a card, on which was handprinted, in bold capitals:

Supporters of the world unite,
Rest in peace from Wednesdayites.

This re-drafting of a mythical expression of people's unity, symbolized the common theme of the hundreds of poems that arrived in Sheffield during those two or three weeks in the spring of 1989. Professional football has often been the context of violent division and a violent form of inner-city communalism. Here were poems and an outpouring of mass cultural action that demonstrated the opposite.

The grief found a narrative form from those who had been there and felt an irrepressible compulsion to tell of what they saw and experienced. As a 13-year-old boy declared:

> Survived I had. It can't be true,
> Got to tell them what I'd been through.

And that is what he did:

> The mood of festivity was soon to quell,
> When the gates were opened to the Tunnel of Hell.
>
> Carried along on a tide of despair,
> The shrieking fans all gasping for air.
>
> Got to get out, Dear God, please out.
> In desperate panic I started to shout.
>
> Then all was ended, all was dark,
> Some time later stretched out on the park.
>
> Someone was holding me, begging me, 'Breathe!'
> 'Don't have to beg mate, can do it with ease.'

We never discovered if such poems were born of lived experience or imaginative empathy. It didn't matter, for there was a mass elision of both which achieved a common authenticity. Yet for the families of those killed, there was still an almost unimaginable expression of pain, of those whose senses have lived and re-lived the human impact of sudden and unprovoked loss with an absolute totality. A man wrote to his wife, who died alongside all the others:

> Our colours lie unmourned
> Gathering dust in forgotten drawers
> No more to wear on Glory Days
> We'll never stand to watch
> Shirts of red on grass of green
> Or shimmering trophies
> That glitter and gleam
> In springtime sun[2]

The harrowing testimonies of professionals were also thematic: a poem about a young football supporter comforting a weeping, distraught policeman; a clergyman's account of suddenly seeing the bodies of the fallen young supporters in a makeshift mortuary; or a Sheffield nurse's anonymous poem, 'For a Liverpool Supporter I Tried to Revive':

> You made me promise you wouldn't die
> Well, now you know I told a lie.
>
> I didn't even know your name.
> I'm sorry my efforts were all in vain.
>
> So, if you're looking down from heaven above,
> You will know I send these flowers with my love.[3]

All these couplets of pain, agonized simple rhymes and stanzas of bewilderment and immense pathos, signified a huge collective release of public and private emotion, but much more too. They were messages of love through plain and obvious poetical devices, attempts to help and support through words and forms with which all could identify, and all could understand. An 11-year-old boy, Mark, from Sheffield, expressed it with a disarming lucidity in his short, unrhyming poem, 'Help Them':

> Help them forget what happened
> Help them get through this disaster
> Help them recover from this tragedy.
> Help them forget that awful Saturday.
> Help them all.

This was not poetry as therapy: that was far too narrow and shallow a description. It was poetry of solidarity between the bereaved and those who wanted to be with them. It was also poetry of unity between the people of three great English cities, symbolized by the managers of their football clubs, who had provided brief introductory messages at the beginning of the anthology. From Brian Clough, a Yorkshireman at Nottingham: 'Words can't replace anything – especially lives – but they can help, and I'm delighted that this anthology is being produced by Sheffield City Council. It stands as a moving tribute to those who died and their love of football.' Ron Atkinson, manager of Sheffield Wednesday stressed the working-class history of football, and declared that 'those people who died loved football, and the best memorial we can give them is by promoting the good and positive things on and off the field, which will ensure this great people's game of ours is equipped to retain an important role in the lives of ordinary men and women for generations to come'. The more laconic Kenny Dalglish of Liverpool added his thanks, emphasizing the 'thousands of messages of sympathy, many expressed in a poem', which Liverpool Football Club had also received, to commemorate the lives of its fallen supporters.

Many of the poems developed a theme of inter-city empathy and unity –
an antidote to all the communalism and violent rivalry between opposing
supporters which had been a feature of professional football over the preceding
two decades. A Sheffield woman wrote to the people of Liverpool, quoting
the club's anthem:

> Oh that our two great cities
> Should be joined through tragedy,
> Oh how could this have happened
> Things like this should never be.
>
> We're a city built on seven hills,
> We made our name from steel.
> And though we're strong and firm,
> Our hearts are warm, we feel.
>
> So people of dear Liverpool,
> Don't feel you're on your own.
> And when your dreams are tossed and blown
> You'll never walk alone.
>
> And so I didn't dream it all,
> But a nightmare it will be.
> Today, and each tomorrow
> And through eternity.

And an anonymous Liverpool poet sent in this poem to 'The People of Steel':

> We've travelled from Anfield, the reason we came,
> Was to tell the people of Sheffield,
> That they were not to blame.
>
> Tho' our homes and hearts were torn apart,
> To thank you all – is so hard to start.
>
> The kindness you showed to us
>   On our sad day,
> Will never be forgotten, forever
>   Day by day.
>
> So when you come to Liverpool
> And we all pray you do,
> We'll welcome you with open arms,
> For 'Sheffield, we love you.'

Such poems were simple and formulaic in the sense that they employed
birthday card rhymes and rhythms, but they meant everything to those who

wrote and received them – they expressed huge and popular emotions. School-children wrote them, mothers, fathers and pensioners too, and often you could not tell the age group, there was such a jelling of content, form and sentiment. A Mr T. Cain of Liverpool expressed this transmigration of friend-ship and love in terms of his city's river, its history and longevity:

River of Tears

There's a river whose fame was the trade it did bring.
It brought the world's bounty where a city did spring.
But now flows another which bears our worst fears.
　　Its colour is sadness
　　It's a river of tears.

The Mersey is old now, and well past its prime,
And how it may serve us, we'll see in good time,
The other's more recent, though it could run for years,
　　Its movement is solemn
　　It's a river of tears.

We'll sail the old river and make the heart glad,
Our children will see it, and know what we had.
But the river that sweeps us, all merriment clears,
　　Its taste is of heartbreak
　　It's a river of tears.

Sheffielder Frank Taylor was among a group of steel-city people who walked across the Pennines to Liverpool, collecting money for the memorial fund. This odyssey was put into verse as:

We walked side by side for mile after mile
Collecting cash, which made our journey worthwhile.
The road was long, the slog was hard
Each step that was taken seemed like a yard.
Through towns and villages, cities as well
The cash we collected began to swell.

When they arrived in Liverpool, they were escorted to the Kop end of Anfield Stadium,

There we stood in silent prayer
It was hard to believe we were standing there.
A deadly silence hung all around
As we stood to face the football ground.
The silence was broken as a loud-hailer said
We'd arrived from Sheffield to honour their dead.

There were other consequences of the tragedy that created a righteous anger. The tabloid presentation of the events included an assertion that the Liverpool supporters themselves were to blame, that they were drunk and unruly and provoked their own disaster. There was no evidence for this, only scurrilous hearsay and prejudice. The reporting in the *Sun* provoked a Liverpool-wide boycott of all the Murdoch newspapers, as Steve Qualtrough recorded, in his short poem 'The Setting Sun':

> Today I saw the eclipse of the Sun
> Because nobody bothered to buy one.
> The stand was piled high with copies none bought,
> I hope Rupert Murdoch is distraught.[4]

And in her 'Ode to a Gutter Reporter', Liverpool poet Peggy Appleby developed a theme of critical literacy in the deadly wake of the events:

> Slimy creature, scavenging over bodies not yet cold,
> Drooling as he contemplates the stories to be told.
> He looks like a man but he's not quite whole.
> His mind is twisted and he has no soul.
> He can't understand, he has no emotion,
> A mother's love, a wife's devotion.
>
> He counts the bodies and hopes there'll be more,
> He rubs his hands, a great story to be sure.
> He hears there's a little boy, his search goes on.
> To him it's a body, not some parents' son.
> He hears of little girls, young and old men,
> This frightening creature starts searching again.
>
> He hovers around bodies for identification,
> He then goes off, to harass relations.
> Telling lies in big bold print,
> He piles on the dirt, he doesn't stint,
> Harassing mother, father and Gran –
> How can this creature look so like a man?

Remember Hillsborough provoked the spirit of a 1989 *Lycidas* a thousand times over. But how do you categorize the beautiful lyricism so direct from the heart, of a woman who writes from the very family of the bereaved?

> Adam died at Springtime,
> When I could see the cherry and apple blossom
> From my window
> When the season showed such promise
> And life lay all before him
> The future and the laughter.

When the book was published, we organized a public launching from within the Mandela Room of Sheffield Town Hall, inviting the parents and families of all those who had been killed. Many schoolchildren read their work, but parents and grandparents read too, and footballers. Nigel Pearson, the then captain of Sheffield Wednesday, read with a moving dignity the words of 'We Remember', by a Manchester poet, Fiona Durlaston:[5]

We Remember

I stand facing you; I am clothed in red,
You are clothed in blue,
That is the only difference –
The colours that we wear.

Suddenly the noise ends,
The volume turned to nought.
We stand facing each other
In silence.
The tears begin to slowly fall down my face
They drip,
Then form a flowing river of sorrow.

We will never forget those we lost –
Our collective family.
But their memory will live forever
In the life of the game,
Of football.

Many Liverpudlians crossed the Pennines that day, locked in sadness and memories. But poetry had also caused a certain oneness between separated cities and communities who hitherto had known very little about each other. The secretary of the Hillsborough Families Support Group, Barry Devonside, who had lost his 18-year-old son, said: 'Everyone on Merseyside is grateful for the love and concern shown by others since the disaster. This book is a moving tribute, and we can only say, thank you.'[6] Their struggle for a true and just public understanding of the tragedy continues, even to this day.

But the last words of *Remember Hillsborough* move from sadness and mourning to critical insight and the assertion of hope and understanding which are the subliminal messages of the tragedy. As 13-year-old Sheffield schoolboy Nick Hinchliffe wrote to conclude his poem 'Afterwards', remembering the words of the greatest of Liverpool's managers:

Bill Shankly's words:
'Football is not just a matter of life and death.
It's more than that' –
Are wrong.
Life comes first.

Notes

1 See 'Words of Grief and Tribute', *Working for Sheffield*, 28, Sheffield City Council, May 1989. Unless otherwise acknowledged, all the poems quoted are from Chris Searle and Steve Chew (eds) *Remember Hillsborough*, Archive Publications, Runcorn, 1990.
2 From *Words of Tribute*, an anthology of 95 poems written after the Hillsborough tragedy, 15 April 1989. Liverpool University Community Research Unit, 1989.
3 From *Words of Tribute*, ibid.
4 From *Words of Tribute*, ibid.
5 *The Star*, Sheffield, 11 April 1990.
6 *Yorkshire Post*, 12 April 1990.

10

VALLEY OF WORDS

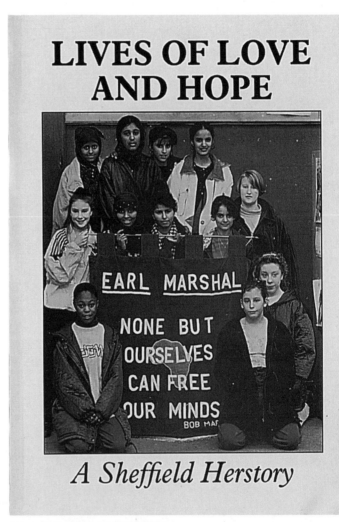

Cover photograph by Stefan Arend

Shortly after I was appointed as headteacher to Earl Marshal Comprehensive School in north-east Sheffield in 1990, the city's chief education officer, who had been on the interviewing panel, was telephoned by an official at the Department of Education in London, and advised not to ratify the appointment, because, he asserted, I was too much a radical, too much a risk. Being a man of independent spirit and strong progressive views in the reforming tradition of Sir Alec Clegg, he paid no heed, and I began working at the school in September of that year.

A small school with rapidly declining rolls, its teachers were divided between forward-looking colleagues who wanted to make it a genuine hub of the local community, and those in a mindset of the fear of change and a trepidation before the knowledge and cultural richness of the communities the school served. One-hundred per cent working class, the families around the school comprised the most internationalist school constituency in Sheffield. By 1995, 83 per cent of the students were from the local Pakistani community (mainly from the Mirpur region of southern Kashmir), from Yemen – both south and north – from northen Somalia, where they had fled from the cities of Hargeisa and Burao after the violent government repression during the civil war in 1990, and from the Caribbean. This was an exceptionally vibrant and worldly-wise community; a 13-year-old Jamaican girl characterized it in this way in 1994:

School of the World

In a big city
In the country of England
In the bottom of a valley
Is . . . a school building.
Although the city is Sheffield,
The building is not all Yorkshire,
For it has a whole nation in its walls.
There are Black Caribbean people,
Yemeni, Somali, Pakistani and white.
Some whose parents have
Struggled and fought to get here.
They have even been in refugee camps
Cramped in a small space,
Terrified of the soldiers,
But they have arrived here
To come to this school,
All with one desire to learn,
Whether black, red, yellow or blue.
Whatever the colour or size,
The school's strong principle says:
'None but ourselves can free our minds!'

Anita[1]

And an 11-year-old white girl also wrote about this human amalgam in Fir Vale, Sheffield:

The school of the world is in the valley
The school of the world has different cultures
Its people have different languages
Its people have different life stories
The children all get along together in peace
The school of the world has children that come
From all different places in the world
The school of the world is a friendly school
The school of the world taught me everything I know
The school of the world taught me how to love others.

Amber

The huge motivation of an education for their children, as well as work and the betterment of life which had driven the parents and grandparents of this community to come to Sheffield and work in the lower-paid jobs of the city's declining steel industry in the 1950s, 1960s and 1970s were the strongest and most compelling of forces. A Yemeni boy, recently arrived in 1994 after the civil war in his country and the destruction of his family house in Aden, wrote in his new-found language:

Learn!

Because
           I want to learn
I travelled thousands of miles
I watched the skies and the moons
I left my beloved family
           oh yes I did
I did because I want to learn
I want to be somebody
I want a nice future
yes I do
           yes I do
I did it all
           because I want to learn
                   I want to learn
I cannot wait to succeed
I cannot wait
no, I cannot
but I must
           I must learn
with my brain!

Wiel

Above the valley where the school lies, a large rounded hill, Wincobank Hill, was the 2000-year-old site of an encampment of the Celtic Brigante people, who had resisted the armies of the invading Roman Empire. So Fir

Vale was a place of much history and much resistance, and its new communities powerfully continued those traditions, through language especially, for the neighbourhood thrived in its multilingualism. Any walk along its streets would be an experience of hearing Panjabi, Arabic and Somali as well as a variety of South Yorkshire and Caribbean dialects of English, all at work.

One of the first tasks I was set by the school governors, and one I took on with a particular enthusiasm, was to work on and change both the founding principles of the school and its profile. We adopted a new logo: three doves, black, white and brown, soaring upwards from an open book above the watchwords: 'For excellence and community'. At the foot of our official printed letter paper was a line from Bob Marley's 'Redemption Song': 'None but ourselves can free our minds'. These words were to have a particular resonance for many of the students as they began to gather their true and strong meaning. One day Nohman declared in a poem about education:

> Something that you can be proud to show to the world
> That's what you'll get with Education
> Education will get your life moving
> so remember
> 'None but ourselves can free our minds'

There were some teachers who objected to both the new logo and the watchwords, caricaturing Bob Marley as 'some Jamaican drug addict' whose words and example should have no place in any school. They also supported the previous logo – a heraldic lion, the emblem of the Duke of Norfolk, the 'Earl Marshal' to the monarch, after whom the school had originally been named as he had owned the land upon which it was built. As time went on, such differences were to take on new implications.

Almost as soon as I had taken up my new post, the Gulf War began. This had a particular significance for many of our students because they became the targets of the increased racism against the Arab, Asian and Moslem communities in England that it provoked, but also because a particularly strong and growing school constituency, the Yemeni community, were directly involved. Because of the new, unified Yemen's refusal to become a part of the US-led multi-national force that came together in Saudi Arabia to coerce a 'military solution' on Iraq, the Saudi government expelled all Yemenis working in Saudi Arabia, and dispatched them back across the border. The economic disaster for Yemen as a nation, and for individual families like those of our students now without the remittances they depended upon, was immense. There was also the potential for a deep problem of communalism inside the school, as different cultural groups within the school took up contrary positions towards the belligerents. Some saw Saddam Hussein in a heroic light, others felt quite the opposite and strongly supported the US- and British-led forces. The Yemenis were in a situation of committed neutrality, upholding the rights of the Arab peoples to find an Arab solution.[2]

Yet out of the danger of division came its opposite. We used 'English' lessons and assemblies to exchange positions openly, within a dialogue of equals, and gave particular importance to the experience and knowledge of our Arabic-speaking students, many of whose families lived in or had direct knowledge of the nations around Iraq (Jordan, Syria, Saudi Arabia and Yemen). We invited parents from the Arab community to come to the school and discuss the issues with the teachers who had no living experience or understanding of the roots of the war or the historical regional differences. In the classrooms, poems and stories were written as acts of empathy, trying to understand the minds of the combatants. Money was raised to help Iraqi families of medical students at local universities caught out by the war, and an Iraqi mother, very affected by the generosity of the students, gave the school a beautiful sequinned tapestry with the words of a sura from the Koran. Out of war came words of understanding, human solidarity and peace. As Mohammed Kassim from the Yemeni community wrote and read at an assembly during the height of the war:

> Why is the world always in war?
> Why do the rich hate the poor?
> Why can't the whiteman love the blackman?
> Why can't they be friends, what don't
> > they like?
> The meaning of peace they don't know
> If they did they wouldn't have war.
> Peace isn't just shaking hands
> It could be facing up to peoples' demands . . .
>
> But no!
> They want to rule what is not theirs.
> They make excuses and support millionaires.
> If only they could stop and think on their demands,
> Maybe war could stop and they could shake hands
> Peace could stop killing in the sand.
> Peace could remove the gun from the hand
>
> Solidarity is the way we should live today,
> And together as one stand up for our say![3]

The new founding principles of the school also had their detractors and opponents among a number of the more conservative teachers, who felt that they gave far too much power and encouragement to control the school to students and community.

Founding principles of the School

Excellence and High Expectations
We expect nothing but the best from our students and their teachers. We encourage them to aim high and maximise their effort towards high

levels of examination and academic success, maximum attendence and all-round achievement. We expect them to be ambitious and eager to learn.

Commitment to our Community
Our school belongs to the community which surrounds it and is served by it. We encourage the highest possible community use of our buildings and resources.

We are committed to extend further the uses the community can make of the school and its resources, and to move both policy-making and governance towards active community involvement and representation.

Friendship, Cooperation and Respect
The school can be successful only if its atmosphere and work are guided by friendship and cooperation between students, students and teachers and between school and community, with the commitment to growth in self-respect and respect for all and between all. This involves:

1 Pride in our internationalism and respect for the life-experiences, languages and cultures of all school members and their families, all citizens of Sheffield, a great city with a powerful past and a dynamic future which all must have a share in shaping.
2 An active opposition to any form of racism or cultural arrogance. We are equals in all aspects of our humanity, and our school must serve as an example of racial justice, intercommunity cooperation, understanding and respect.
3 A pride in the achievements and potential of our young women students and a determination that all their ambitions can be realised. Also a respect for all women colleagues and the powerful contribution they make to the life and development of the school.
4 A commitment that the able-bodied and disabled work together in friendship and equality for the benefit and greater education of all.
5 That the friendship of equals can grow between people of different generations: that teachers and students work together as cooperators with mutual respect and self-criticism, without authoritarianism and with an understanding that they can learn from each other and with each other for the benefit and education of all.

Democratic Development
Our school needs to be the centre of community democracy, which encourages discourse, debate, difference and divergence, all within the spirit and development of a critical literacy. To these ends the creative energy of our students, arising from the variety of their languages, cultures and life-experiences need to be valued to the full in structures of democracy, such as school councils. Their involvement in the life and changes of the school needs to be encouraged by their participation in school forums and developmental structures.

Respect for Guidelines and Reasonable Conduct

The guidelines and rules informing school conduct need to be observed by all, and guided by the school's Founding Principles.

Anti-social behaviour, indifference towards or refusal to complete the tasks of study, disrespect for others, unpunctuality and truancy, aggression towards peers, verbal and physical bullying, disruption of lessons, dishonesty, victimisation, vandalism, domineering or selfish behaviour, insults and name-calling or making other students' lives anxious and painful – all are habits which are destructive, intolerable and have no place in the school.

Reward and Emulation

Constructive conduct should always be acknowledged and praised; achievement by students and teachers recognised and commended.

A system of encouragement of positive achievement will be developed whereby examples of success in and constructive contributions to the academic, cultural and social life of the school are projected as worthy of emulation. This practice will be part of the school's daily life, both in and out of the classroom.

I quote these principles in full, partly to show the thinking and ethos behind the new conception of the school and the stand that it was taking, and partly because of the centrality of critical literacy and creative pedagogy within the school. It had to withstand considerable difficulties: the local education authority proposed its closure in 1991, shortly after I started as head-teacher, and it was only through the broad and intense support of the local community and students, and their committed campaign, that it managed to survive. The multilingual banners expressing the school's determination to stay open, all under the symbolic message of the new logo, carried the meaning behind the school right through the community. When a long-time leader and activist of the Pakistani community declared at a campaign meeting that the school was 'the second home' of those who lived within its neighbourhood, he could not have expressed its aspirations more truthfully or poetically. Its buildings had become the venue of a large-scale community education development – a weekend Arabic community school organized by the Yemeni community with up to 180 students meeting Saturday and Sunday, a daily Koranic and Urdu class run by the Pakistani parents through the mosque, a Somali women's class and an ambitious cricket centre organized by local Caribbean and Pakistani cricket enthusiasts, following visits to the school by the Pakistani captain Imran Khan and the Jamaican-born, Sheffield-bred England fast bowler, Devon Malcolm (after whom the centre was named).[4]

Perhaps nothing excites so much cultural action and protest within a struggling community than the threat of losing its school. The school, if it is living up to its purpose, is the centre of that community's cultural life and aspirations, the venue of ambition, intellectual growth and the promise of knowledge as power. As Faheem, one of the students, made clear in a campaigning poem:

I've been at Earl Marshal for over a year,
And I'm not moving, I'm staying right here!
To close a school for good
You'd need to padlock the door,
But if you do
You'll be asking for war![5]

And his classmate Matthew set down his reasons for fighting to save the school in his own way, directed at the local education authority:

You say you'll shut down our school in 1992
But who are you?
We have many cultures in our school –
Somalis, Pakistanis, Asians and Yemenis,
Not only do children use this school
Adults and parents use it too.
We have a Youth Centre and a Sports centre too
Without these things what would the locals do?
So put these thoughts into consideration,
Just stop and think before you ruin our education!

Some poems read like ready-made slogans and became their own banners as they were read out in assemblies, campaign meetings, over the radio and in the classrooms:

We'll do more than fight
To get our equal rights.
If you're asking for a fight
You'd better think twice.

In Shameem's sharp rhyming, there was wit alongside will:

Asians, Somalis, Saudis, Syrians, English and Yemenis –
We all come to this school, and we're not enemies.

In a host of letters sent to the council, in the lyrics of songs of protest, in radio and newspaper interviews and delegations to councillors and education officers, the critical and campaigning literacy of the students was employed and tested. And it reached out to the community too. A local grandmother and ex-forklift driver in a now closed-down steelworks, visited the school, spoke to the students and went away and wrote her own poem to them. Two verses went thus:

When I first made a visit here
And met you and some of your tutors,
For the first time in years I began to think
That there was some hope for the future.

> And these school-closing maniacs,
> You could teach them something too,
> Maybe you could help them see the light.
> 'Cos I'm sure if they spent a few hours with you
> They might get their priorities right.

When the news finally came through that the campaign had been won, we organized a multilingual celebration, inviting all those in the immediate and wider community that had helped and supported us. A rainbow of words was set free that evening, as the students read, performed and sang in all their languages, and 14-year-old Marie listened proudly as her Pakistani classmate recited a 'victory poem' she had written:

> Today's the day
> Our good news reigns.
> You people here
> Have taken pains
> To save our school,
> And see it shine.
> 'Can't stop us now
> We're in our prime!'

While the school worked hard to improve its examination performance (by 1993 it had achieved the best GCSE examination results for many years), it also developed its own school and community publishing initiative, producing between 1992 and 1995 four major books which presented the creative writing of the students. *Valley of Words* (1992)[6] included work on multilingualism, poetry about their families and communities, their response to the Gulf War, the struggles of black South Africans, Palestinians and the Kurdish people, and poems written as part of the campaign to prevent the closure of the school. This assertion and extension of the students' internationalism was also very much a part of the second book, *Lives of Love and Hope: A Sheffield Herstory* (1993),[7] which brought together a number of oral histories of the students' mothers and women in their families, telling of their lives, their childhoods, their experiences of marriage, migration, resettlement, war and domesticity, and often of their determination for education and greater freedom in their lives. These 'herstories' were supplemented by poems and stories by the students, most of which identified with the struggles of women across the world. Some particularly moving poems expressed the terror of women incarcerated in the 'rape camps' of Bosnia:

Bosnia Poem

> It's not my shame
> It's theirs.
> It's not my shame
> I was the victim!

They think the rape has made me weak
but it's made me stronger.
They feasted on my body
They ate every morsel
They think they've left me hungry.
Then why is it
I am full of anger?
Raping us Muslim women
has shown their weakness!
Letting tears stain our faces
has shown their cowardliness!
Us women have left our homes
We've screamed and told of our suffering,
and yet we still say:
'It's not our shame –
                                    it's theirs!'

Sufurah

A series of very moving pieces concerned the death of 10-year-old Yeliz Arslan, the Turkish girl who died when her house was fire-bombed in Molln, Germany, by neo-nazis. Asma, from a Bangladeshi family, wrote this poem in the last section of *Lives of Love and Hope*, dedicated to Yeliz:

Yeliz' Last Thoughts

Never could understand why,
Why they do this.
Never could understand their brutality,
Why are the people's minds so cold?
Never could understand the Swastika
Why they said we must die.

Never could understand the skinheads,
Why blood stained their hands,
Never could understand hatred –
Why was their hope that we should go?
Never could understand their fascist salute,
Why was it aimed at us?

Never could understand the slaughtering,
Why we had to end this way.
Never could understand anything,
Why we had to live this way.
Never could think of their minds
Why were they so cruel?

Never could understand people –
Why could they never understand?
Never could understand what we have done wrong,
Why do they kill us with firebombs?
Never could understand Hitlerism,
Why did it have to rise again now?

Asma

The preoccupation with 'understanding' the nature and causes of violent racism provoked the writer of 'Yeliz' Last Thoughts' to conduct her own survey on racism in the school and neighbourhood, which she submitted as part of her GCSE humanities examination. It gained widespread interest and publicity, and helped the school to assess and develop a strategy against the weight of the problem both internally and externally. When a busload of football supporters from Sunderland passed through the neighbourhood of the school on the way back to the motorway from a match against Sheffield Wednesday in 1992, and made insulting gestures and racist insults to local people out of the window of their coach, a group of students, including the writer of 'Yeliz' Last Thoughts' wrote a letter of protest to the club. Sunderland's manager, Malcolm Crosby, wrote a letter of apology to the students and the school, which was read out during assemblies.

Lives of Love and Hope was eventually shortlisted for the Raymond Williams Community Publishing Award, sponsored by the Arts Council of Great Britain, and was widely read, reviewed and used by teachers and university lecturers in the United States and Australia.

I have written at length about the 'herstories' and their vibrant, moving and deeply educative narratives elsewhere, and it would be demeaning to offer short quotations or précis. They need to be read in full, and it needs to be understood that they were produced by means of a long and considered process. The students interviewed their mothers, grandmothers or aunts, usually in their first language, truly their 'mother's tongue'. Then these interviews were translated into English, edited, given to their teachers for corrections and further suggestions, edited and re-edited until a final draft was produced. The result was intimate words as intimate history, but also a history beyond childhood, motherhood and domesticity. A history that embraced resistance to anti-colonialism, and remembered civil war, the mass movement of whole peoples, migration, settlement, racism and new forms of struggle in a new land. These are the insights from a powerful review of *Lives of Love and Hope* by Adele Jones, in the international journal *Race and Class*:[8]

'I was born in Hargeisa, Northern Somalia, with a developed sense of responsibility.' The opening line of one women's story from *Lives of Love and Hope* gives an indication of the restrictions, expectations and responsibilities that are linked, it seems, inextricably, and yet inexplicably, to her being a woman, even as she was born. But, in this collection of stories of the lives of women, there is no resigned acceptance of the limitations, whether created by circumstances or the expectations of others, imposed upon them. As the title of the book aptly states, the lives of these women, who live in Sheffield but who originate from distant and diverse lands, are lives of love and hope. They are also lives of frustration, ambition, anger and rebellion. As Asad's mother, born in Khanabad, Pakistan, tells her story, it is the rebel that shouts the loudest, despite, or perhaps in spite of, the daily struggles she deals with.

The main section of this book tells of the stories of women of different nationalities, but mainly from working-class backgrounds. In narrating these to their children, the women demonstrate the value of oral history. The children, in turn, through the process of transcribing and editing, have added their own touches of wit and humour. One young person has succeeded in creating the impression that her mother's pregnancies were an inevitable consequence of her father's journeys to and from England! 'He kept going to England, staying for a few years and then went back to Yemen, and every time he went back to England she was pregnant.' And the dryness of northern humour is revealed in this account of a dog leaving home: 'When I was little we had a dog and the dog had a mongrel puppy. My dad said it would have to go and it got up walked straight out of the house. We never saw the dog again.'

The women's stories, time and again, expose racism and sexism, yet show that their lives and dreams are more than just a response to these. Descriptions are unambiguous and to the point. 'Farooq was a lousy creep,' states one woman as she builds up a picture of the oppressive marriage she is in and then, in language which evokes dignity and strength, she describes Farooq's mother. 'There was Farooq's mother. She was a wonderful woman with a proud nose and mouth, sturdy arms and black bushy hair tied in a bun. She never wasted words, but would smile quietly instead of speaking. She had a large, extremely strong body which had borne her twelve children and strong, wise eyes which had seen four of them die.'

In these lives, hardship and struggle are real, not romanticised. Mowahb's mother: 'I was born in 1959 in a small village in Yemen called Asirhh. I have had a difficult life. When I was about nine years old, I learned how to cook and how to get the water. You couldn't believe that I had to walk about 8 miles to get to the water! I had to wake up at 3 or 4 o'clock in the morning to make the breakfast, and then go to get the water.' It is these simple sentences that explain the emotion I feel when I see picture postcards which, in catering to the voyeuristic interests of tourists, commodify images of young women with water carriers on their heads. Similarly, there is nothing romantic about the struggle of Fozia's mother to save her family from war in northern Somalia. The continuing tragedy is that, having fought for refuge in England, she is now fighting racism.

The pattern is clear, these ordinary women, in defining and describing their own experiences, neither glorify nor reduce themselves. They are who they are. Black women, familiar with media images that equate Asian with 'exotic', Caribbean with the 'domineering black woman'

– shoulders so broad she can carry anything – and African with the passive and grateful receipt of aid, powerfully assert that they are who they are. White working-class women, too, present images drawn by themselves, not as others choose to portray them. They are who they are. These women will not be confined to the boundaries imposed on them. In talking about their lives, they link the past with the future. This inter-generational dimension creates the context in which they live and reminds us, as in the song by Sweet Honey and the Rock, 'that the dead and the unborn are linked to the living'. One woman explains: 'I am not sure where the story of my life begins. I think it must begin before my birth and to understand my life it must be necessary to know something of my parents' lives and the lives of their parents also!'

Some of the stories provide an historical account of colonialism. The mother of Safa describes the British occupation of Aden, in Yemen; the man she married was in fact blinded at the age of 16 while fighting British soldiers. When she came to England, Safa's mother came 'to see the country which had occupied us for such a long time.'

Environmentalism is another issue touched upon in the book. The difference here is that it is not reduced to the purchase of green soap, but is about the relationship of people to the land that sustains them and the impact of environmental changes. There is an account, for example, of the changes brought about in one woman's life and in the surrounding villages by the building of the Mangla Dam in southern Kashmir. Her experiences are set down without judgment as to whether or not the dam should have been built; after all her life without electricity would have been difficult. The content of these stories is thought-provoking and demonstrates that, for as many ways as there are by which women are kept down, so as many ways will be found through which they will fight back. Cassie's mother, white, working-class, 'brought the union in' to her employers to challenge a rule that women who married would be dismissed. Not that Cassie's mother had any plans to marry, it was the sheer injustice of the rule that she was fighting. Marsha's mother, on the other hand, a black woman from Jamaica, used education as a means of fighting back and successfully obtained a degree while working and rearing a family.

At the back of the book is a section entitled 'Daughters'. Through poetry, short stories and personal accounts, young women express their anger at racism, war and hurt. The power and talent emanating from these pages is humbling. Naeeda Razzak, in her poem 'A Somali Refugee', questions the 'civil' in civil war and in 'England, a civilised country'. She finds only meaningless violence, whether in the deaths in Somalia, or the racist taunts on the streets of London. The poems of protest about occurrences in Bosnia have a significance that has no geographical, religious or even 'ethnic' boundaries. The young women also pay tribute to Yeliz Arslan, the 10-year-old Turkish child who was murdered by firebombers in Germany. In writing on these topics, they will have faced the fact that there is often an expectation that the writings of Black people, and of women in particular, will be overtly political. This is also sometimes presented as a criticism of Black writers. We know, however, that we can only cease to protest against oppression when there is no need of protest. What is important is that we document our own experiences and find our own voices of expression. That is precisely what this book does.

School of the World (1994),[9] the next publication, gave a full opportunity for the students to express the huge vitality and breadth of their internationalism – not only in terms of their own family and community origins, but also through their imaginative empathy and reaching out to other citizens of the world in places as far apart as Soweto, Hebron and Kashmir. A Pakistani girl, for example, expressed the determination of an elderly South African woman voting for the first time in a meaningful election, her democratic intention unbuckled in the face of violent racist intimidation:

I Wasn't Scared

I was walking with my grandchildren,
A bomb exploded right behind me.
I didn't run
I wasn't scared
I walked ahead
Knowing I was going to get to the polling station.
Before my death
I will vote!

Shaista

Such poems about a post-apartheid South Africa had followed many creative efforts in the years before which sought to understand with solidarity the struggle of young people in the townships during the last years of racist rule. Poems like this one by Naeeda, which showed how a word can mean entirely different things in different social and political contexts:

In Detention

I'm in detention
For not doing my homework.

They're in detention
For crying for freedom.

I'll be home in two hours
They'll be home in two months
Or maybe more.

They might not even come back.
They'll be tortured,
I won't.
They'll be hanged like clothing
I won't.

How many lives
Will be lost?
How many mothers will shed tears?
How many loved ones will die,
Die before Africa gets its
           freedom?

Naeeda

Poems such as these were not simply routine classroom or 'English' exercises: they were part of a process of 'knowing.' They came out of the study of relevant texts, the mounting of exhibitions on Kashmir, Yemen and the Caribbean composed of artefacts, newspapers, photographs and pictures borrowed from homes. There were also the visits of writers and speakers. Trevor Huddleston, now 80 years of age, came to the school from London to tell of his visit to post-apartheid South Africa and the changes he saw. The South African novelist Mandla Langa visited, as well as the Jamaican novelist Joan Riley, the Pakistani author Rukhsana Ahmad, the Guyanese poet John Agard, and local poets, musicians, dancers and writers were frequent visitors and performers. There was an electrifying performance of Nigerian dances by the Port Harcourt University dance company, and dances composed and performed on the spot by our students and members of the Zimbabwean Sunduza dance company. Weekly African dance tuition was given by a talented dancer and artist from Guiné-Bissau. The cultural action around the students' writing was also connected to their fund-raising work. Between 1990 and 1995 they raised funds for the Imran Khan Cancer Hospital in Lahore, Pakistan, for the victims of floods in Bangladesh, and to help rebuild shattered school buildings in Hargeisa, Somalia. Through sponsored events, sales of food and clothes, collections in the neighbourhood of the school and organized sporting and cultural events from cricket matches to fashion shows, they contributed towards medicines for the Kurdish people, and raised money for victims of cholera in Guyana, for the upkeep of stranded Iraqi student families in Sheffield during the Gulf War, for refugees from Bosnia, and for relief efforts in Kashmir, as well as providing thousands of pencils for literacy students in Ethiopia. In all this work they used their wit, inventiveness and huge commitment, and allied it with their creative imaginations and powerful use of words.

When the students heard, for example, of the struggles of the Kurdish people in northern Iraq, they raised £200 through sponsored swims and silences. When the Kurdish doctor, Dr Risgah Amin, visited the school to speak in assemblies to tell the students about the plight of his people and receive the donation, he said that at one time he thought that the only friends of the Kurds were the mountains which gave them shelter and protection – but now he knew they had many young friends in Sheffield too. And Nahid, having studied the Kurds' situation and the poison gas attack at Halabja, read her poem about the irrepressible Kurdish dream:

Under the Black Blanket

We Kurds are under the black blanket
And the rest of the countries are under the blue
We dream of a country of our own,
A dream which someday will come true.
An Iraqi once said that I shouldn't dream,
It isn't good for me, and it's hard to be true.
I said to him, 'a dream doesn't hurt!'
He said, 'it will hurt if it doesn't come true.'
Why are we under the black blanket
And not under the blue?
Why is it so hard for us to dream?

After some hard work fund-raising for the Guyanese people, the donation was presented to representatives of the Guyanese community in Sheffield. Three months later the school received a letter from the President of Guyana, Dr Cheddi Jagan, who had been deposed as the chief minister of the then British Guiana in 1953 when I was a boy, for his 'communist' leanings. It was an unusual and uplifting experience for the students to read these words on the embossed and headed stationery of the office of the president of Guyana:

I have been deeply moved by the concern and personal efforts displayed by the first year pupils of the Earl Marshal Comprehensive School. I wish to personally put on record my sincere gratitude to these future women of tomorrow for their significant contribution, which by no means is small. This demonstration of unity and individual involvement reflects positively for future generations. Their example will inspire others and will no doubt be duplicated. Relatives of persons affected by cholera and the victims who benefited from the efforts of these youths I am sure, will ever be grateful to them.

School of the World also contained a long chapter about 'journeys' – stories of visits and sojourns made by the students to their countries of origin, and narratives of migration that they and their parents had made in order to arrive in Britain and, finally, Sheffield. There was some skilful, humorous and harrowing writing here, the stories of returns to places from Curaçao to Brunei, pilgrimages to Mecca, holidays in Kashmir and the river states of Nigeria. Nabat, from Burao in northern Somalia, wrote openly of the terrifying events that had caused her family to flee to relatives in the Somali community of Sheffield. This was not 'Mortal Kombat' or the cybernetic death fantasies of computer games. Suddenly this was about real people like Nabat herself, as she stood by the side of her friend who read her story during a morning assembly.

> Then the war came to my town Burao and it was like a slaughterhouse. Wherever you looked you saw dead people – women, children and the old ones. The houses were all knocked down and bombed. There were hardly any walls or roofs, and big holes were everywhere. People were blown up by mines sometimes, and they lost their legs and feet. The side of my body was burned and scarred by the fire of a bomb. All the lights were out at night, it was all dark. You could only see people's eyes gleaming. It was frightening for us, like a long, long night that was never going to end. The government soldiers came into our houses and killed the men and raped and whipped the women. They took my cousin Farah who was 22 and they cut his arm across the wrists and they made us watch him when they killed him. All of us were crying, we never stopped crying. They said to us, 'If you go, we're going to kill you!' Then they raped his wife. All this I can never forget. I still dream about it, then I wake up from my sleep and I am shouting. I still hear the bazookas and the explosions as the shells hit our houses.

Such truths, such moments were a part of our school and the words it generated – real words, real lives – the world learned through words striking the senses, through these languages in this valley of words. There was Anis' journey too, to Aden: he thought and hoped, for a holiday to see his family. He found himself in the middle of civil war, bombardment and the devastation of his city.

> At first during my visit to Aden it was peaceful – just as I expected. There was no war. I went to the seaside with my old friends. The beach was crowded and the sand was almost blue. Later I went to the Red Star School to meet lots more of the friends I had known before.
>
> Then one Wednesday, at about eight o'clock at night, the war suddenly started. The shelling and the bombs were terrible. There were explosions all around and explosions overhead, just like I imagined that the Second World War was like. People were screaming and running all around, and some were hit by the blast and pieces of exploding buildings. There was blood in the streets and suddenly the buildings were looking like ruins. Everything changed – even the weather looked changed too and it became much more hot and sticky. Whole families were killed and I saw people with their arms missing and even one man with his head blown off.
>
> So I went to help in the hospital, bringing water from the tanks to the old people who couldn't walk. There was no water in the taps and we had to bring the water back to the hospital in big bottles. There were not enough doctors and not enough beds. People were lying on the floor and some of them were dying and bleeding. Some were groaning and crying for their lost children, only thinking about their families and those they loved.

Education could not have been more actual, more authentic when Anis' friends read all this, written by their friend in the classroom. Suddenly there was a truth in what they were hearing about the world 'out there' – their world, – from a boy who sat next to them. We had a way of recognizing the courage shown by Anis in his home city. We awarded 'Peacemaker' certificates to students who took initiatives or helped organize events that had peaceful or cooperative ends, and which created reconciliation or prevented conflict among students. Students who sparked and organized fundraising events, who stopped fights or worked against racism or communalism within the school or wider community were our 'peacemakers' who were formally presented with a certificate at special assemblies. So Anis received his, with the citation that he had 'shown the eternal qualities of friendship and making peace with others, the hallmark of a true and generous human being'. The words across the bottom of the certificate read: 'The cause of peace is the hope of the world.'

There was much too in the 'journey' narratives that was more gentle, poetical and full of marvel. There was Nadia, who had just read Anne Frank's diary and who wrote daily messages to Rehana, the name she gave her diary during her holiday in Pakistan. Or Afroz' wonder when she first saw the Holy Mosque in Mecca: 'I couldn't stop looking at it. I mean it was so beautifully clean and neat. It was shining from all over, and half of it was made of real gold.' Or Earl's surprise at seeing the awesome beauty of the Jamaican countryside: 'There were running rivers and trees everywhere, and all through the countryside there were houses built on the sides of gullies and cliffs as if they might fall over at any time.' Or the moving story of the much shorter journey, the last one Lorraine took to visit her dying grandmother in Chesterfield. It was all there to know and share, to make a community of friends out of a school of the world – for that was the ultimate objective of our critical literacy.

That it all hinged on languages, an affirmation and equality of all languages, the students knew well. All around the school those languages were free to speak, free to share, free to learn. The proclamation of the school's sure future, which had been asserted in all the languages of the students during the campaign to keep it open, became a harbinger of language pride and development. Khadeegha wrote about 'My Arabic Language':

> Words of my language are expressive and dear to me.
> That's how I feel about my language.
> No matter how far I go
> No matter where I am
> I'll still think of my precious language . . .

> My language
> My heart is throbbing
> My heart starts to beat more
> when my language is mentioned . . .

Izat wrote in English and Urdu, spoke in English and Punjabi. He composed a poem about what he thought was the power of his words:

> Speak the language you were born with,
> Show your feelings to the people around you.
> Show the people you are proud of your language.
> Language is a great thing,
> With language you can make friends.
> People will know you as long as you live.
> Language can help you to understand things around you.
> Language can make you proud and happy
> Language will lead you to happiness
> Don't let anyone make fun of your language,
> Shout your language out to people around you!
> Let them know that you love your language
> And you will speak your language as long as you live.
> So shout your language out!

Izat died a few months after writing this poem. He had a weak heart and had been under hospital care for most of his short life. Afterwards, his classmates helped the textile teacher make a beautiful banner which we hung in the main resources area of the school. Over a picture of Izat, and his name and the years of his life, is his line, boldly and proudly lettered:

SHOW THE PEOPLE YOU ARE PROUD OF YOUR LANGUAGE!

Yet many of the students knew too how cruel words could be. The same words that could open up the world could also close it down with messages of hate, violence, racism or sexism. The constant campaigning within the school to use language in all its positive, loving and learning functions was often undermined by its use as a tool of terror, threat and discomfiture. As Nadia wrote in her poem, simply called 'The Mouth':

> I am the mouth
> I am the mouth that the teeth are in
> I am the mouth that the saliva is in
> I am the mouth that contains all those words
> I am the mouth that says all those hurtful words . . .

In this context, the projection of counter-words of dignity, of meaning and friendship was vital. Hence the emphasis on suspending words on walls, sewing them on banners, reading them out in assemblies, giving them back to those who owned them in a form of respect and recognition, sharing them as messages of achievement in published books – it all demonstrated powerfully the true and sharing uses of language and the beauty of words.

This sharing took on an especially vivid and moving form in the 'Poems to Quddus'.[10] Quddus Ali was a Bengali youth from East London who had been set upon and badly beaten in the Commercial Road, Stepney, in a racist attack by some white youths. His head had been kicked against a kerbstone. He had gone into a coma immediately after the attack, and stayed in that condition for three months until Christmas Eve 1993. When a large group of his supporters, predominantly Bengalis, organized a peaceful protest outside the hospital where he lay, several were arrested by the police: nine were charged and they became known as the 'Tower Hamlets Nine'. When we discussed and studied these events in our Sheffield classrooms, with information gleaned from newspaper articles and campaign materials, the students empathized deeply, knowing the realities of racism themselves from their own lives in and around Fir Vale.

Many wrote their poems to Quddus actually imagining themselves, like him, in a coma – as if they were experiencing a stream of consciousness in their minds. What would he be thinking, deep inside his mind? It was a brave act, to imagine in this way. Anita imagined him returning to Bangladesh and its riverine landscape:

Quddus' Dream

Why are my eyes going dim
And why is my head hurting me?
Maybe it's death I'm in . . .
No! I can see a river,
Its shining waters flow by
And all the pretty flowers
And the sun is in the sky
Maybe I'm in Heaven
Or maybe on an island,
Now I can see a ricefield
This place looks familiar,
Perhaps it's Bangladesh, my homeland.
There are no vehicles or cars here
The air is fresh and clean.
Maybe I'm in a time machine,
Gone back to the first days of creation.
I can hear my mother calling me,
I go back home
I look in the house –
She is not there, but I can hear her.
She is crying and telling me things.
I don't understand what she is saying
My eyes are going dim again
I can feel something on my hand.
My eyes are getting lighter,
I can see a glimpse of my father
He sees me smile at him
Suddenly he runs out to call the nurse . . .

Hey! This is not my bed,
Where am I? What am I doing here?
I try to get up
But my Mum gives me a hug
She says I was in a coma.
My head is hurting again.
I think I am going back to see the river,
I can't see my Mum anymore.
Maybe it's better for me to be here watching it
Until the sun goes down forever.

The indignation of the Sheffield students poured out of some of their poems, as in this one by Farooq:

Quddus and the Nine

He is lying there like a dead body
Trying to fight for his life
He knows what's happening outside
He can feel the pain over and over again
Like a bad nightmare.
His friends are opening a campaign
To fight for their rights
To defend themselves and their families.
Then the police came,
Hitting whoever came their way.
Nine teenagers were arrested,
And all they did was defend themselves.
Quddus is still in hospital
And if he dies
And if the nine go to prison,
Then there will be no such word
As JUSTICE.

The meaning behind Quddus' agony was also seized upon by white class-mates. In a quasi-surreal passage entitled 'Invisible', Daniel explored the East Londoner's adventure in a nightmare:

I woke up! I seemed to be floating on an invisible bed. I climbed down.
I was in an all-white room with fog swirling around me. I was dressed in
a white robe, pretty short. Then my family . . . I could hear them calling:
'Quddus! Quddus!'
I saw a door, it appeared out of nowhere. I ran towards it, but . . . Slam!
It banged open and four white youths with devils' masks on walked
through. The masks were smiling kindly, but the faces under the masks
when they were removed, weren't.

The biggest said:

'Welcome to the House of Sin!'

There was darkness and there was light. I was fully clothed, walking down a street. It looked familiar. I saw some youths coming towards me. I'd got it! I was trapped in a nightmare. Then just before I got hit, I was somewhere else. I was in an ambulance. I could see someone on a stretcher. It was me! But no one seemed to notice me, I was invisible. More darkness. I was back in the white room again, the white room was my mind. I could hear and see my parents but I couldn't talk to them. I got back onto the floating bed and fell asleep exhausted.

And Adam wrote a letter to Quddus. We typed it up on school letter-paper, and sent it to Quddus, with copies of all the other poems and stories dedicated to him, for him to read when he woke up:

Dear Quddus

My name is Adam and I am a white boy. I think the attack on you was terrible and I could have thought what it is like to be kicked and punched and to have been called racist names.

I hope you get better. I thought how your parents felt, just seeing you lying there nearly dying. I hope you are out of your coma soon and I give you my best wishes. And I think that the police should be arrested, and not your friends.

I can imagine how you feel, you are just lying there nearly dying and your friends are at your side, sticking up for you! You can't hear them, you're just lying in your bed having a dream about the attack.

Quddus' story provoked such interest and solidarity that we wrote and asked his campaign organizers to send some speakers to Sheffield to speak to the students in their classrooms and answer any questions, and also to address parents at a public meeting at the school on the evening of the same day. They came. The students read their poems to the two young men from East London, and asked many questions. During the parents' evening meeting they performed their poems again, to the delight and approval of the parents present. The poems were also read to students in schools in East London by members of the 'Tower Hamlets Nine' campaign group. Thus young people from two great cities in the south and north of England met through their words and through Quddus, their cause.

In July 1994 I took a group of 20 or so year nine students to London for a few days, stopping at a city youth hostel. Most of them had never seen London before. We walked around the West End, viewing the usual sights, but spent the final day in East London, in Spitalfields and Whitechapel, before going on to the Tower. Some of the students wanted to visit the world and streets of Quddus: he was still in their minds. As we walked up Brick Lane, I remembered the lines of Tony, one of the *Stepney Words* poets. His had been one of the real and 'gloomy' poems that riled the social complacency of the Sir John Cass governors, 25 years before:

> Brick Lane is a horrible place
> Where everyone has a gloomy face,
> There isn't one little space to play football.
> Everyone plays in the dirt
> Filling all their hair with dirt,
> What a place.
> I always try to be happy and cheerful,
> Now I begin to get doubtful.

After returning to Sheffield, the Fir Vale students wrote their own poems about their sensations of London. I gave them no literature to stimulate them, but asked them to write about the places we had seen and the streets where we had walked. Zulfiqar wrote words that seemed to me like ghosts:

Brick Lane

> Brick Lane, a lane of pain
>   for some.
> Brick Lane, a lane of destruction
>   for some.
> The West End is a treat for some,
> The East End is a beast for some.
> While the West End makes money
> The East End goes broke.
> I walked through the West End
> I walked through the East End,
> I saw the differences.
> The money in one place
> The poverty in the other.
> Brick Lane, so quiet that morning
> As if the Black Death had returned
> But with the racism of the BNP
> This time it has changed its colour
>   to White.

Farooq's impressions too were as if they had come from the mind and agony of Quddus. Writing again about Brick Lane, 'near the place where Quddus Ali was attacked', he continued:

> The next day I went to the East of London.
> As I saw the life around me
> I didn't know if the place was London or not.
> Most of the shops were barred up
> To stop the racists breaking the windows.
> There was broken glass
> From the shop windows.
> There were mainly Asians there.

Then when I went past a notice board, it said:
'Don't vote for the BNP'.
As I read it, then I knew
Racism had captured life there.

Such events gave our students not only increasing confidence to publicly express their poetry and the empathy and insight within it, but to reveal their feelings and understanding of the racism and injustice around them. After the visit of the campaigners from East London, it seemed as if some of the reticence had been lifted away. As one poet wrote:

Racism is like a word chucked out of hell –
if hell can't cope with this word,
How will we on Earth?

Shasim told a tale of shopping for clothes for Eid (the Muslim festival celebrating the end of the fasting mouth of Ramadan) in Meadowhall, the huge shopping complex outside Sheffield, built over the site of a famous steelworks – ironically the original lure and reason for so many of the school's families living and working in Sheffield:

Black Dresses

Eid was coming up
I was excited to go to Meadowhall
To buy myself a long dress.
I saw a white dress,
It had embroidery at the top and bottom,
Small black flowers inside.
It was nice, so I bought it for £10.
As I left the shop
Five white boys came out of the arcades.
They pushed me about
As if I'm not a human being
But some kind of dirt.
They snatched the dress off me
They told me white wasn't the right colour,
So they put the dress in the mud
They swung it over my head
Then handed it over to me.
The dress was all ruined,
I cried, it hurt in my heart.
One of the boys told me to 'look there!'
I looked into the shop
There were plain long black dresses.
They told me to wear those on Eid.
I left the muddy dress
I wiped my tears

I walked along the empty streets
And came home in the darkness.[11]

What to do when words carve out such cruelty? It is when words are the
harbingers of action, linked to doing, and the confidence that gives rise to
doing, that their true meaning emerges. *School of the World* contained many
such moments as those described so poignantly and simply in 'Black Dresses',
and moments of action and resistance as well, as in this poem by Sadakat,
who, like many of his friends at the school, was part of the protest of Asian
youth outside Attercliffe police station in May 1994, after a group of young
Bengali men were arrested by South Yorkshire police.[12] They had been attacked
by some local white men, but not unusually found themselves as the ones
harassed, accused and charged. Sadakat's words express his own sense of pride
in actually *being* there, of holding the banner, of being an active part of a
group of people who are not accepting, who are fighting back:

Outside Attercliffe Police Station

Everyone was there last night at the picket.
Fighting for their brothers
Fighting for their freedom
Fighting for their religion
Fighting against racism
Fighting against the whole of Attercliffe
            Police Station
For their brothers who were arrested for nothing.
I was feeling strong to see my younger brothers there,
Fighting against the racist people.
The road was blocked
The flags were up and flying
I could see about six hundred people
      jumping up and down.
Up and down
For their younger brothers,
And on the flag it said
NO JUSTICE, NO PEACE!
It took a lot of strength to hold those flags
In such a windy place as Attercliffe.
That's what I saw last night,
And I was there too!

It took the same confidence and courage for Wiel, a Yemeni boy from a
refugee family in Aden only two years in England and still grappling with the
language, to read his poem publicly to passers-by on the steps of Sheffield
Town Hall. He was there with his family, members of Sheffield's black communities and a delegation of Somali and Yemeni refugee students from his
school. They were protesting in December 1995 against the government's
new Asylum Bill which threatened to remove benefits such as family credit,

housing benefit and free school meals from families appealing for the right of asylum. At that time we had about 80 students in the school threatened by this impending law, and a group of 16-year-olds had already organized an impressive fashion show in their dinner hours to raise an emergency fund, in case the law was passed and the refugee students suddenly had no way of paying for their daily school lunches. Now Wiel and his younger cousin Shemsan recited this poem, passing the megaphone backwards and forwards to each other as they read alternate lines with clarity and passion:

Orphan of War

Yesterday my father was killed.
The day before yesterday, my mother.
Today I am an orphan.
I want to cry but I have no tears.
I am only a child
I am only a child.
Someone please help me.
I want to cry
I want to cry
I want to cry
        but I have no tears.
I want to live
I want to learn
I want a home.
        Where is my love?
        Where is my family?
This is my life
This is my future.
I am alone
I want to cry.

The same cry and message of internationalism, combined with the school's commitment to peace not only within itself, but also in its community and in the national and international dimensions, came from the students in the lower school who took part in the 'No More Hiroshimas' campaign. In 1995 it was the fiftieth anniversary of the atomic holocaust of Hiroshima and Nagasaki, and we were determined to mark and remember it. We set aside a day for workshops on the themes of the nature of the disasters themselves and their continuing consequences: 'Japan today'; the stereotyping and caricaturing of Japanese people; art and 'haiku' poetry sessions arising from the Hiroshima experience; and an evocative slide-show of the tragedy and its aftermath. In the afternoon we turned to a five-a-side football competition refereed by the young Sheffield Wednesday footballer Chris Bart-Williams, who had been born in Sierra Leone, came to London as a child, and shared many of the same experiences of linguistic and cultural adjustment with our own students. There were eight teams, each one representing a city which had been devastated by bombardment and war: Hiroshima, Guernica, Dresden, Coventry, Hanoi, Grozny, Sarajevo and finally, Hargeisa in Somalia, the home city of many of our Somali students. The significance of the names was made clear to the students, who supported their 'cities' with placards, slogans and words of encouragement. 'Guernica' won the tournament, but it was a victory for all who had taken part, learned and understood.[13]

Meanwhile, parts of the school had been covered with poems about Hiroshima, written by students who had read closely and internalized the account of the events in John Hersey's *Hiroshima*.[14] Two Pakistani girls became the delta land itself where the city stood:

> I am the land where Hiroshima once was
> > a city,
> I'm the land where buildings once stood,
> I'm the land where flowers and trees
> > used to grow,
> I'm the land where children played,
> I'm the land where babies stood and cried,
> I'm the delta land where seven clean rivers
> > once flowed,
> I'm the land which is no use now,
> I'm the land which isn't noticed any more,
> I'm the land which is bare now,
> I'm the land which is lonely now,
> I'm the land where hideous corpses lie,
> I'm the land of Hiroshima.
>
> *Retsana and Fozya*

And two boys, a Pakistani and a Yemeni, took hold of a fascinating Japanese word, *mizu* (water) and built a poem about Hiroshima around it:

Mizu

> 'Mizu! Mizu!'
> Say the people of Hiroshima,
> 'We want water!'
> A man comes to help,
> He jumps onto a sandspit
> Of one of the rivers of Ota.
> He looks around him
> And hundreds of people are saying
> 'Mizu! Mizu!'
> He says, 'there is no clean water,
> The water is poisoned,
> And the only clean water
> > runs down your face.
> It is your tears.'
>
> *Ghamdan and Fiaz*

Words, in whatever language, messages to consciousness, leaders to action, coming from all directions. A quotation from the Koran, suspended on the walls near 'Blessed are the Peacemakers' from the Bible, provoked a telling poem from Shahid. He was considering the words: 'O Mankind! We have created you male and female, and have made you nations and tribes that ye may know one another'. His poetic response, particularly his last line, became new watchwords for the school:

> *Know!* What does that word mean?
> It's something which no one has seen
> It's something deep in someone's heart,
> It's a spot on their body's part.
> Whether man or woman.
> Different nationalities and different races –
> It's when you understand each other.
> Gradually growing, it turns to friendship.
> Caring for and loving others.
> Nothing can stop us knowing each other
> As day by day we increase our knowledge.
> Without the word *know*, the world is a
> disaster.

Knowing the world means knowing yourself, using the word to know yourself in a process of understanding guided by self-criticism and the criticism of those you trust and respect. In a school such as Earl Marshal – in conventional terms at the top of the list of 'deprivation' and 'special needs' – it was vital that both students and teachers did not become engulfed in a deficit ethos of 'cultural disadvantage'. There were huge cultural, linguistic and creative advantages to the life of the school – the deficit was in economic terms and in terms of opportunities and resources. As I was quoted as saying at the height of the events that finally led to my 'removal' from the school in December 1995:

> The issues of inner-city education will never be resolved while we look upon these remarkable and vibrant children as problems. Most know at least two languages and two cultures at the age of twelve or thirteen. We must respect their intellectual power and ambitions. They are much more world-aware than the ignorant people who talk about them and hand them down their curriculum prescriptions.[15]

Yet the complexities of our students' lives often led to distress, anger, disruption and indiscipline, frequently manifested during school, often because it was the easiest place to demonstrate a personal rebellion. Other schools had disciplinary processes which ended in the expulsion of students. In these circumstances gaining admission to another school was very difficult – for some students downright impossible, although as a school we regularly admitted many students who had been expelled from other schools in Sheffield. Expulsion meant the risk of a fast track to criminalization, a daytime and night-time life on the streets, the temptations of burglary and shoplifting in the neighbourhood or city centre shops or the lush and tempting shops and gambling arcades of Meadowhall. There was also a serious drugs trade on the streets around the school, and the expelled or truanting student became easy prey for those controlling it. So the position that I, as headteacher, and the governors took was that we would not expel unless the circumstances were completely impossible and all the possible creative approaches had been exhausted.

One of the emphases that we took as an alternative to exclusion was *writing* – to use the *word* as a way of hastening self-focus, self-recognition and self-criticism. This approach was developing in an increasingly hostile and divisive school situation, as a large wedge of the teachers were very unsympathetic to the school's 'no-expulsions' policy, and were not cooperating with it. Some teachers were actually provoking students into trouble so that they could then argue that such a policy could not work, and the only 'sensible' expedient would be to expel them.[16] Many of the writings in such circumstances, with students upset, angry, rebellious, wronged or guilt-laden were intensely personal. But in the context of a violent confrontation, a fight, argument, an incident of bullying or name-calling, one of my or my colleagues' first reactions would be: 'Write about it, get it down, write what you feel and let's study it, learn from it, see if it can help us find a solution'. Sometimes this writing would take an autobiographical form, with the student looking back over her or his life. There were, for example, heavy pressures and lobbying from some teachers for the expulsion of this boy whose brief life-description follows. He had great difficulty in writing, so I have followed his own punctuation and spelling to demonstrate how his struggle to write about and know himself was possibly a part of his distress. Even so, he manages a certain clarity and eloquence:

> I was born in 1978 Dec 24 I usta go to nershery and then I went to beck road then when I lived around pitsmoor I went to the advensher playgrond and got beten up by some ashien boys and girls and I had to black ayes and something els. I have lived in matlok sheffield worksop all over and my mum has got cancer and then my dad got sent to prisen for somthing he did not do I think I went to Berngrev Middle School and I was Geting pick on by a lot of people and If I had fight whit one of them and I got blemd for cosing trubbel whit some of the peaple at Berngrev Middle School now I am at earlmarshal hompreyhemsif school And I play a lot of football and I am playing to night I have playd football for this school and we drew 1–1 I like P.E. and enjoy runing when my leg is not hertin I think the wers thing that has happend to me is caling names and being reasis and not being like in this school because of that but I am going to put a suden stop to all the name calling that has been going on in this school.

Such writing encourages dialogue and makes counselling easier – there is a text provided, a use of the word to lead and clarify. There are also the beginnings of a self-knowledge: a critical literacy of the self. In the following passage this self-knowledge has become strong and sophisticated with the words and their insights becoming its levers:

I am writing to express my feelings, I always express my feelings on paper. It's hard to do things you want to do when you're black, muslim and a girl, especially at my age. My life is very confusing. I know they say to me, 'Fatima you're a very bright girl'. I know this, and so do you, but I do not like being treated different. The more people tell me what to do, the more I rebel, and this is a fact, I cannot help what I feel, but I feel like fighting for my own rights. I try very hard to be good, I *am* good but I am at the wrong place at the wrong time. I have *no* freedom at all. I go to school, from school I come home, no spare time because at school I have teachers looking after me, at home my parents, and sometimes my brother. I have grown to love my culture and religion, but I have been put on this planet 'Earth' to do something, but I feel I'm not going anywhere, with this constant talk I hear about me. I am treated different at home because I am a girl. My father is sexist, he chooses what he thinks I should do, and as far as I know my future isn't in University as you know and I think it should be. My future with my father is me getting married at the age of 15 and going to where he was born I think is unfair. How good or bad my behaviour or personality is this is the way my dad sees my life. And when I think about this I think about my future and sometimes I wish I wasn't born. I sometimes think I was put on this planet to be tortured, for wrong and fight. This is not my fault, but I want to have as much freedom as possible, before my future is wasted by my father. I feel different from everybody, I feel disgusted at myself when I get into trouble, but I blame it all on my father. Why can't my life be the same as anybody else's? Why am I getting picked on? I sometimes look outside the window and see Muslim girls about 18 or 19 going to college to learn. I ask, why can't I be them? I feel like running away, but running away from problems leads you to more. I am writing this to you and you are the first to know about my feelings because I trust you to be on my side, because it seems to me that everybody is against me. I am my own best friend and I trust nobody but myself, and I hope you will understand what I'm going through. This cannot be a phase, this is real *problems*, and I hope you could stop them, or more problems will occur. I think every night of living in a big mansion, and I smile to myself. That is how I try not to think of my problems. I think of other good things, my feelings of anger and hatred have been going on for quite a long time. I'm sorry if I've bored you with problem after problem, but if I keep them to myself I know they'll get worse.

There is a sense of catharsis here, but much more. The writer is seeking to use words to know herself, to look upon herself critically but rationally. She lays blame, but she also finds reasons. Words are helping her, they are her friends – for in her frustration and loneliness she has relied upon them and they are coming back with clues and some answers.

In some situations, students in 'trouble' went directly into poetry. Perhaps the question of finding a form, a shape, a pattern, a frame helped them – perhaps it was the 'flow' that poetry can encourage. Here, a Caribbean boy, a regular truant, addict of arcades and another candidate, in the minds of many teachers, for expulsion because of his frequent 'disruption' of lessons, asks himself a question through his poem: what will his situation be when he leaves school, if he carries on in the same way? He answers by putting his poem in the context of the Yemeni cafe in the neighbourhood of the school, where he frequently disappeared in school time in order to play on the machines:

Cafe

I'm unemployed
I never listened to my Dad
or anybody.
I had the choice
when I was twelve,
I had a feeling
I wouldn't pass my test,
but I never listened to myself.
I went in the cafe
when I started this school
and I kept going in.
One of my friends
took me into this cafe,
Since then
because of the arcades
Playing those machines every day
I can't come back out from it
unless I have no money left.

The final book published at Earl Marshal was a further anthology called *Heart of Sheffield*.[17] This had a particular resonance for me, because it connected with a theme of things *local*, and it was almost as if the ghosts of *Stepney Words* were rising from the students' poetical insights about their neighbourhoods in north-east Sheffield: Fir Vale, Page Hall, Grimesthorpe, Pitsmoor and Firth Park. There were the same naked and vivid statements of discontent about the streets, houses and prospects:

Fir Vale

One day I went to the fortune teller's
And I asked them, 'what's the fate
                    lying for Fir Vale?'

There are going to be a few good fellars
There are going to be a lot of drug sellers
A person in prison
A person on bail
Many children here are going to fail –
That was the fortune teller's tale.

Hanif

Or Sajida's commentary:

Fir Vale

I was lying in my bed
And I was looking at a book
        I had just read.
It was about a very nice place called Fir Vale –
Well, according to the book, anyway!
It was so different from the real Fir Vale
It had clean and tidy roads
No smashed windows covered with boards
There wasn't any litter
And everyone was much, much fitter.
Children were playing
Their parents were praying –
Then I thought about the real Fir Vale
And litter on the streets
Parks without any seats,
People being called racist names
And no children playing any games.
What kind of a place is this?
It's a place you can never miss.

Retsana and Nazia entered into the soul of an abused and vandalized street:

The Street No One Cares About

I am the street of Idsworth Road
I am the street which has got broken
                  bottles on it.
I am the street that has a pub on it.
I am the street where muggers hang about,
I am the street where people shout,
I am the street where dogs bark,
I am the street of troubled people
I am the street of Idsworth Road.
I am like a prisoner
People dump things on me,

They don't know I have a life.
I can feel the children play on me
I can feel the heat of the sun
I can feel the pain
When glass bottles are smashed on me.
I am the street of Idsworth Road.

The poem of 25 years before, 'I think Stepney is a very dirty place / But I like it', came back to me as I read Naveed's poem about Fir Vale:

Our Part of the City

Our part of the city
Might not be the best.
It might not have
           the best buildings,
It's got a lot of traffic
But it's our part!
People being friendly
Being kind and loving –
It's not a quiet part
But it's our part!
There might be an odd burglar
Or an odd gangster
But it's our part!
It's our part of the city!
People playing football
People playing cricket,
We like our part of the city!
Our love is for different people,
They might be black or white,
For us they're all the same.
It's a good part of the city.

In so many poems, the students – most of the writers were between 11 and 13 – drew dramatic distinctions between the vandalized, littered and depressing environment, and the vibrancy and friendliness of the people who lived there:

the people of the streets
     are warm and caring,
when you're down they give you
     loving

For there was strength there – as Jabar insisted:

I see different faces and races,
And they're all strong in their mind.

For whatever the economic or environmental pressures, there was pride that:

> it's an area of culture and tradition,
> people from all over the world
>   make it a community.

And as the final poem powerfully asserted, partly through a prophecy-like warning, partly through an exhortation:

> we must build up our own community
> A community of peace
> A community of understanding
> A community of relationships.
> But if we are too busy drowning
>   in an ocean of hate and crime
> Then our communities will split away
>   and become separate continents
> And our blood will become a sea
>   of a multicultural colour
> And in the end there will be
>   a world of mist and darkness
> where apartheid must rule,
> a world that is sinking down
>   into a gutter of death.
> So if you want more of a life,
> then build unity in the community.

The menace of drugs was often invoked in *Heart of Sheffield* as it had been in *Stepney Words* – it could hardly be otherwise as trafficking and addiction was becoming an increasingly serious problem to local people. As a school we had a policy of dealing openly with the issue. We often took students who had been expelled from other Sheffield schools because of some drug-related behaviour, and sought to counsel and prevent, not to condemn. When a 15-year-old boy passed out in the lunch room, having taken a concoction of dangerous substances in a street near the school, we used the incident to draw attention to the problem, rather than cover it up. We worked closely with the boy's family and called a community meeting at the school to formulate a local plan of action against the drugs menace. A particular danger to everyone, especially infant children, were the increasing numbers of discarded syringes left around the unwalled campus of the school in the evenings, or on the plots of waste ground nearby. In one class we read a story from the local paper about a child picking up such a needle, playing with it and putting it to her mouth, while her horrified mother ran to her to remove it. This had a strong effect on the class, and its members had similar stories to tell. One girl, 11-year-old Sarah, wrote this:

I am the syringe
that you find in the street.
I am the syringe
that attacks you on the waste ground.
I am the syringe
that pricks you and kills you.
I am the syringe
that you should stay away from.

I am like a live snake
that gives you a bite.
I am like a live wire
that gives you a shock.
Stay away!
Or else you will have
a very short time to live!

What does it feel like
When you leave your child
standing on the waste ground?
and I prick her –
What would you do
When your child is infected?
What would you do?

This became a theme poem of the school's anti-drugs work. It was read out in assemblies, studied in classes, published and performed by its young author at city-wide events. It was a most efficacious and useful example of critical literacy and a spur to action – writing at its most starkly creative, but also at its most concrete, most connected to real living and a campaign to oppose and prevent a growing evil.

These were some of the ways writing became the prompter of deeds and wider social acts at Earl Marshal between 1990 and 1995. In December of 1995, my time was over – the local education authority did not like the ethos or direction of the school, and Ofsted, the national inspectorate, labelled it as 'failing'. Some of their criticisms of genuine weaknesses were valid, and we were working hard to rectify and improve them, but they also criticized the school's curriculum and ethos for being 'unbalanced', 'neo-Marxist', and having too much emphasis upon things 'non-European' and too little that vindicated a 'harmonious' view of history and an adherence to the 'National Curriculum' and things European.

I have described the precise events that led up to my ousting and the arbitrary removal of the powers of the school's governors elsewhere.[18] The students resisted through a boycott of classes and demonstrations outside the entrance to the school. They produced leaflets, contacted the press, television and radio and spoke eloquently on regional news programmes. The governors struggled hard against the manoeuvrings of the local education authority, which used its powers to take their powers and their school away from them. I returned only once, for a farewell assembly, a month later. The students played a song which resounded through the otherwise silent school theatre. I caught some of Labi Siffre's thematic and determined lyrics:

> The higher you build your barriers
> The taller I become.
> You can deny me
> You can decide to turn your face away
> The more you refuse to hear my voice
> The louder I will sing –
> No matter
> Because there's something inside so strong,
> Something inside so strong.

After I had spoken and given my thanks and goodbyes, Yahya, a Yemeni student who had been less than two years in the school and in England, stood up. He had written one of the poems in *Heart of Sheffield* which declared:

> We have brains, we can stop them,
> I can, you can, we can
> with our brains!

Now he spoke in his own language, reciting by heart some lines in Arabic by the Palestinian poet, Mahmoud Darwish. I have no knowledge of Arabic, but a colleague who was present who had, told me that it could be translated into English as:

> Where should the birds fly
> After the last sky?

I thanked him and left.

But that was not the end of the story and its words. A certain spirit of resistance seemed to have taken over these young people. In May 1996 they were on strike again, boycotting classes as a protest against an assault on a Yemeni girl and alleged racist behaviour by a teacher. As the Sheffield *Star* reported: 'Scores of pupils went on strike. Police were called as banner-waving students protested at the gates.'[19] Then in July after the appointment of the new headteacher and the virtual takeover of the governors by local education authority appointees, a decision was taken to change the logo of the soaring black and white doves, and replace it with the former heraldic lion, symbol of the British aristocracy who stole the device from Africa, and the emblem of the Duke of Norfolk, the 'Earl Marshal' of England. One day the students saw on school letters home to their parents that the switch had been made without warning or advice. Gone too were Bob Marley's words from 'Redemption Song'. The last night before the end of the school year they got to work. When the students and teachers arrived for the final day they found inscribed on the school entrance and the walls beside it, and along the road leading up to the main building: 'None but ourselves can free our minds' and the shapes of the rising doves stencilled on the walls. The students were holding onto their words. They would not let go.

Through the school year that followed, they campaigned for the reinstatement of the doves. In their introduction to a petition sent to the new school governing body, the local education authority and the headteacher, they wrote:

.Many of us feel the 'Three Doves' represent:

- all the communities of the school
- equal opportunities for all races, colours, sexes, classes, abilities
- the power and strength of peace
- learning
- that we the pupils of Earl Marshal can fly high and achieve the best.

The 'Doves' mean to many of us much more than the new crest.

The system was implacable and, unsurprisingly, refused to concede. But the doves were still flying in their hearts, and as they wrote in the messages accompanying their petition:

> Learn to fly
> Let your wings take you where
> you want to be.
> Each and everyone has wings,
> It's just a matter of finding them.
> Let these doves fly as one.

Notes

1 *School of the World*, Earl Marshal School, Sheffield, 1994.
2 See Chris Searle, 'A school and a War', *Race and Class*, 33 (4), 1992, and *Living Community, Living School*, Tufnell Press, London, 1997.
3 *Valley of Words*, Earl Marshal School, Sheffield, 1992.
4 See Chris Searle, 'Towards a Cricket of the Future', *Race and Class*, 36 (4), 1995, and Kevin Mitchell, 'Mean Streets feel the Pace of change', *Observer*, 21 May 1995.
5 See Chris Searle, 'Campaigning is Education', *Race and Class*, 35 (3), 1994, and *Living Community, Living School*, op. cit.
6 *Valley of Words*, op. cit.
7 *Lives of Love and Hope: A Sheffield Herstory*, Earl Marshal School, Sheffield 1994. See also *Living Community, Living School*, op. cit.
8 Adele Jones, review of *Lives of Love and Hope, Race and Class*, 35 (3), 1994.
9 *School of the World*, op. cit.
10 *School of the World*, op. cit.
11 *School of the World*, op. cit.

12 *Star*, Sheffield, 2 June 1994.

13 'Players are all victors', *Star*, Sheffield, 17 May 1995.

14 John Hersey, *Hiroshima*, Penguin, London, 1972.

15 See Tony Harcup, 'Class Action for Poetic Justice', *New Statesman*, 31 May 1996.

16 Chris Searle, 'The Signal of Failure', in Eric Blyth and Judith Milner (eds) *Exclusion from School*, Routledge, London, 1996.

17 *Heart of Sheffield*, Earl Marshal School, Sheffield, 1995.

18 Chris Searle, 'OFSTEDED, Blunketted and Permanently Excluded', *Race and Class*, 38 (1), 1996, and in *Living Community, Living School*, op. cit.

19 *Star, Sheffield*, 21 May 1996.

AFTERWORD

MICHAEL APPLE

Reading *None But Our Words* had an unanticipated effect on me. Its basic arguments about the politics of education and the critical role education can and must play in what Paulo Freire would call 'naming the word and the world' are ones with which I have much sympathy. Yet, even with the power of the arguments, they soon receded into the background. In their place stood the voices of the students, the elderly, the dispossessed, the 'other'. I was struck by the power of their words and by the power of education when it is done in counter-hegemonic ways.

Then something else happened. As I continued reading, my concentration was constantly, and insistently, interrupted by my own memories. Every story Chris Searle told seemed to call forth from the recesses of my mind a sense of recognition. There was a continuous flow of memories of tensions, losses, victories, and struggles to act ethically and justly as an educator in a society where doing so often has serious consequences for those who dare to radically question it.

Since so much of this book is (appropriately) autobiographical, I hope I am forgiven if part of this 'Afterword' takes the same form and I describe a few of the memories that *None But Our Words* called forth.

In the early years of my teaching career – well before I had ever dreamed of becoming a critical 'academic' – I was a primary school teacher in a small and strikingly conservative town in a rural area of New Jersey, a small state in the northern part of the USA. While there was a middle-class population, most of the town was working-class and poor. My own classroom was filled with children who were relatively poor and also with a number of children of migrant labourers who worked on the local farms picking crops for extremely low pay and under conditions that can only be described as inhuman and exploitative. The standard curriculum and the standard textbooks were not only completely out of touch with all of these children's cultures, histories and daily lives, but they were simply boring both for me and for the students in that class.

To try to overcome this, as Chris Searle so often had to do, we reorganized the curriculum. We wrote and performed plays, including a comic opera that the kids themselves created with the help of the music teacher. We studied local history, the relations between food production and the conditions of farm labour, and the hidden histories of the people who were not represented in their texts but who had lived in the area. (For example, the town at one time had had a small black farming community near it that had been a stop on the 'underground railroad' where escaped slaves had been safely housed as they made their way to the industrial cities in the northern part of the state.) We interviewed parents, grandparents and others about their lives and histories there and elsewhere. These were written up into narratives. The texts of their lives became the texts of historical study and led to our going to the archives of the local newspapers to connect the lived versions of historical events with the 'official' news that was published. Histories of racial tensions and racial subjection were uncovered. Histories of racial segregation in the local area (which supposedly never happened in such 'northern' states as New Jersey) were bared. Stories of the uncommon courage of people (white and black), where people collectively and individually stood up to resist racist movements and policies, surfaced as well. The students put out a small informal mimeographed newspaper to tell what they had learned.

As in *None But Our Words*, much of this was 'unsettling' to some people. The local Chamber of Commerce felt that not only were these kinds of topics 'not appropriate for young minds' (the students in my class were 12–13 years old), but also that the things being publicly brought up would put the town in a 'bad light'. This could be 'bad for business'. A local Christian fundamentalist minister who believed that the Bible clearly showed that 'God had made the white race superior' led a small but very vocal group that added to the criticism of what they felt were 'radical' and 'unchristian' methods. Either I was to stop doing this or pressure would be put on the school to ensure that my contract would not be renewed.

Like other teachers I suppose, I was initially shocked by the hostility of these groups to what seemed to me and the students to be simply an attempt to create the conditions for a *serious* education. But after the initial shock had worn off, I decided that I could not let these attacks go unchallenged. I spoke at school board meetings against the racism being exhibited. I publicly demonstrated the quality of the writing and reading that the students were doing and the open-mindedness with which they approached the historical research in which they were engaged. I showed that the scores the students had achieved on the standardized tests were actually higher than before. (Is it so odd that when students are actually engaged in educational work that seems serious to them, they tend to do better at it?) Like so many of the youth whose voices are heard so clearly in this volume by Chris Searle – and in many of the others he has published – the students themselves were not silent about these attacks. They spoke to their parents and to members of the school board, often more than a little eloquently. Colleagues of mine – even those who were more politically and educationally conservative than I was – lent support. They too knew that what was at stake was the loss of autonomy in creating curricula and teaching that were in any way critical. Soon considerable counter-pressure arose. The conservative ideologues had to back down. But for years teachers and students looked over their shoulders whenever methods or content got a bit more 'creative' than the norm.

I look back on this time with both fondness and distress. The students, parents and I had gained – at least temporarily – some important educational space. We had collectively demonstrated that it *was* possible to engage in educational practices that were personally meaningful, that asked critical questions, that were grounded in a sense of critical literacy, and that connected the school to a wider sense of the local community in serious ways. Yet, the fact that it continues to be both professionally and personally risky for teachers to engage in this kind of pedagogic action – and in fact because of the power of the current conservative restoration, may be even more risky at times now – is not something that is the stuff of joy. It is obvious that Chris Searle would agree.

Yet reading Chris Searle's accounts brought back other memories as well, ones that did not have such a positive ending. In *Official Knowledge*[1] I tell the story of one of my most formative experiences as an educator and filmmaker. A number of us were involved in working with a group of young women – all of whom were poor and most of whom were African American or Latina – who were sentenced to a juvenile detention centre. This was basically a jail for young offenders in a rural area of Wisconsin. We were convinced (both politically and ethically, as well as educationally) that employing models of pedagogy based on critical literacy would be considerably better than the 'drill and kill' methods that dominated their school experiences before they had been sentenced, and which were clearly the norm in the limited educational programmes provided in that centre. In a manner similar to what Chris Searle did with poetry, we engaged in film-making with these young women. They made films about their lives inside and outside of schools and detention facilities, and about their experiences, hopes, fears, dreams, etc. Slowly but surely their excitement grew. They worked collectively on visual texts that were both personally and socially powerful and that showed untapped reserves of knowledge, talent, skill, and resourcefulness that had simply been invisible in schools and in a justice system that had all too often come to treat them as 'unworthy'.

The transformation of these young women was immense. To quote one of them, 'Hey man, I'm good!'. Chris Searle's book made me want to get those films out and see them again, to relive that excitement, that sense of possibility.

And yet these memories are crowded out by others involving these same 'girls' (as they called themselves). The administrator of the detention facility wanted us – demanded us – out. We were 'interfering with the smooth running' of the facility. We were 'raising the hopes of these girls'. First get them 'literate' and 'numerate' and *then* they might do a few things that were a bit more 'interesting'. A great wash of anger comes over me as I write these words. I remember the anger of the young women at once again being denied an education that was connected to them. I remember my own disbelief and anger when we were told to stop doing our work there. How could something that so clearly demonstrated that students from oppressed communities, when dealt with honestly and with a recognition of their own knowledge, potential and voice, be 'bad'? What is there to fear from educational experiences that give people power over the creation of their own meanings, and which incidentally make them actually *want* to be involved in education again? These questions underpin much of what Chris Searle has described here.

Of course, answers to these questions are complex. And, if they are not to be thoroughly romantic, they require us to critically examine the economic, political, and cultural inequalities that so deeply characterize both your society and my own. However, while critically analysing the relationship between schooling and both the reproduction of, and challenges to, relations of exploitation and domination is crucial, it also has its dangers. It can serve as an excuse *not* to attempt to create the conditions of critical literacy now. There may be some wisdom in the oft-quoted slogan that goes, 'We must think globally and act locally'. Struggles in education *are* struggles in society.

Chris Searle has brought together a number of stories in this fine book. In so doing, he helps us to restore parts of our collective memory of the very possibility of difference. This is especially important in a time when the rhetoric of efficiency, cost-effectiveness, 'standards' and so on threatens to drown out both the voices of dissent and even more importantly, the voices of students and communities that demand more from their education than rhetorical promises and broken dreams.

Of course, Chris Searle is not alone. Certainly, on my side of the Atlantic there are classrooms and schools where a truly critical education goes on even in the face of withering conservative attacks and a severe fiscal crisis.[2] I am equally certain that on this side of the Atlantic many similar examples can be found as well. These stories need to be told. They need to be made public so that the wave of 'reforms' now being put in place – a return to a more stratified and stratifying school system, a withered sense of school effectiveness that seems to equate education with the metaphors and reality of factory production, and a view of the possibilities of students that is so narrow as to defy the experience of our own lives – can be countered with actual successes on the ground.[3]

Perhaps there will come a time when people like ourselves will be able to read other teachers' stories and not have memories of constant struggle come flooding forth. But until this utopian time comes, we need to listen and learn from each other. We may not always agree with parts of what we hear, but the very act of learning from other teachers carries its own message of possibility. However, listening to each other is not sufficient. As Chris Searle reminds us, we need to listen even more carefully to the voices of our children to remind ourselves of what this is all about. If *None But Our*

Words does no more than have us listen to these voices and restore our faith that a critical education *can* be done now, it will have more than served its purpose.

Michael W. Apple
John Bascom Professor of Education
University of Wisconsin, Madison

Notes

1 M.W. Apple, *Official Knowledge*, Routledge, 1993.
2 See, for example, M.W. Apple and J.A. Beane, *Democratic Schools*, Association for Supervision and Curriculum Development, 1995.
3 M.W. Apple, *Cultural Politics and Education*, Open University Press, 1996.

INDEX

CHILDREN EXCLUDED FROM PRIMARY SCHOOL
DEBATES, EVIDENCE, RESPONSES

Carol Hayden

- Why are there increasing numbers of children being excluded from primary schools?
- What are the characteristics and circumstances (home and school) of children excluded from primary school?
- What can be done to reduce and possibly eliminate exclusion from school?

There can be no more serious sanction taken against a child of primary school age than exclusion from school. We can only speculate upon the likely adverse long-term consequences of such an action, as exclusion from primary school was rarely recorded in previous decades. In this book, Carol Hayden explores the policy context in which exclusions are happening and presents evidence from a two year, ESRC funded national research project on the issue. Accounts from parents and carers, some of the excluded children, as well as teachers form a central part of the research evidence. Possible responses to exclusion from the education service and other agencies are considered. The book provides evidence about *what* is happening, as well as some insight into *why* exclusion is happening with a view to informing practical responses to the issue. It will be vital reading for anyone concerned with the problem of exclusions and will be of particular interest to teachers, educational psychologists, education welfare officers and social workers.

Contents

192pp   0 335 19562 8 (Paperback)   0 335 19563 6 (Hardback)

CHANGING LITERACIES

Colin Lankshear (ed.)

'undeterred by sociological pessimism, Colin Lankshear hacks away at the underbush, clearing a path for a new critical-liberatory discourse'.
James Paul Gee, Clark University, Worcester, Massachusetts.

This book explores everyday social practices and how they influence who people are, what they become, the quality of their lives, the opportunities and possibilities open to them, and those they are denied. It focuses especially on language and literacy components of social practices, asking:

● How are language and literacy framed within different social practices?
● How are social practices in turn shaped and framed by language and literacy?
● What are the consequences for the lives and identities of individuals and groups?
● How can we understand these relationships, and build on this understanding to develop critical forms of literacy and language awareness that enhance human dignity, freedom and social justice?

In addressing these questions the book draws on social practices from diverse settings: from classrooms using conventional texts to so-called 'enchanted workplaces'; from a Third World peasant cooperative enterprise to modern technologically-equipped homes and classrooms. The result is a rich sociocultural account of language and literacy, which challenges narrow psychological and skills-based approaches, and provides an excellent theory base for informing the practice of literacy educators.

It will be compelling reading for academics, teachers and students of language and literacy education, critical literacy, discourse studies and cultural studies.

Contents
Introduction – Part 1: Critical and cultural perspectives on literacy – Language and cultural process – Critical social literacy for the classroom – Literacy and empowerment – Part 2: Literacy and social justice – Language, literacy and the new work order – Appendix: a sample of fast capitalist books – Literacy, work and futures – Part 3: Literacy, new technologies and old patterns – Literacies, texts and difference in the electronic age – Appendix: glossary of technical terms – Different worlds? Technology-mediated classroom learning and students' social practices with new technologies in home and community settings – Conclusion – Afterword – References – Index.

The Contributors
James Paul Gee, Michele Knobel, Chris Searle.
240pp   0 335 19636 5 (Paperback)   0 335 19637 3 (Hardback)

CULTURAL POLITICS AND EDUCATION
Michael W. Apple

Many are convinced that 'liberal' solutions have failed and that answers to social problems lie in a return to conservative policies and values. As this conservative offensive grows increasingly powerful in education, public schooling itself has come under attack. Michael Apple offers a powerful analysis of current debates and a compelling indictment of rightist proposals for change.

Apple presents the causes and effects of integrating schools into the corporate agenda and demonstrates who will be the winners and losers as the conservative restoration gains in strength. Far from defending the status quo, Apple argues that the unresponsive and bureaucratic nature of many school systems has actually pushed people toward the right. 'Yet,' he writes, 'during an era when ... we face the massive dismantling of the gains that have been made in social welfare, in women's control of their bodies, in relations of race, gender, and sexuality, and in whose knowledge is taught in schools, it is equally important to make certain that these gains are defended.' With this dual focus, this book provides an eloquent defense of the possibility of a more democratic public education.

> Michael Apple is among the most distinguished scholars in the world who are involved in the struggle to build a critical and democratic education.
>
> Paulo Freire

> In this timely and provocative book, Michael Apple once again throws light on some of the key issues confronting education ... Apple draws upon contemporary social theory to show how education policy relates to broader societal processes and demonstrates the complex and contradictory nature of current developments in education. ... This is a book that should be read by all educators who are committed to social justice.
>
> Geoff Whitty, Karl Mannheim Professor of Sociology of Education, University of London

> Through the years, Michael Apple has provided us with one of the most compelling narratives we have about the public school in its relation to economic forces, prevailing ideologies, and what Kozol calls 'savage inequalities.' Entering into the domain of cultural politics, he sharpens and further develops his insistence that we consider 'educational reform' within a carefully wrought social context. ... There is hope in this fine book, if we can muster the energy to transform.
>
> Maxine Greene, Teachers College, Columbia University

Contents

176pp   0 335 19731 0 (Paperback)